What are people saying about **Why Should I Hire You?**

WHY SHOULD I HIRE YOU? is definitely one of those books that should be in every potential hire's library. Stephanie's insightfulness in the hiring process is exactly what this 21st century work force needs. Her cutting-edge expertise in Human Resources will benefit any employment huntsman. Stephanie's tips and techniques will help you overcome some of the most common barriers found in the hiring process. Why not make this wise investment and watch the dividends come in excellent hiring stages.

Kimberlyn R. Nelson, President & CEO
The Association of Clergy Executives & Administrative Assistants (ACEAA)

Stephanie C. Harper has created a multi-faceted book, which can be used by employers as well as employees. WHY SHOULD I HIRE YOU? gives readers a fresh and innovative look into the job seeking and hiring process. This book is power-packed with a plethora of information and will be around for years to come. This is a must read for professionals in every arena.

Shunda Leigh, Editor-in-Chief,
Booking Matters Magazine

WHY SHOULD I HIRE YOU? is a must read for those who want to understand the employer's perspective during the career search process. This is no longer something that should be seen as one-sided. Stephanie has successfully managed to help change the traditional job seekers mindset and clearly define the distinction between a job vs. a career."

William Riddick Jr., PHR
Immediate Past President - National Association of African Americans in Human Resources (NAAAHR) - Atlanta Chapter, formerly Atlanta HR Association

What are people saying about **Why Should I Hire You?**

"While employed with ESP, Stephanie was our entire Human Resource Department. She introduced many sound principals that were crucial to ensuring we made sound hiring decisions." WHY SHOULD I HIRE YOU? will make sure job seeker know how the decisions are made.

Eric Berkobin, Vice President, Digital Systems
Electronic System Products

"Many are academically sound, but lack the professional decorum necessary to maximize their potential. I am proud to say, Stephanie provides career strategies that are necessary for transformation into quintessential professionals".

Harold J. Bell, Director of Career Planning and Development
Spelman College

"In this book WHY SHOULD I HIRE YOU?" Ms. Harper has brought a very keen mind, a spirit of excellence and an abundance of Human Resource knowledge. She provides "real-world" insight on career development and presents a unique and beneficial perspective for persons seeking careers as opposed to jobs".

Peter Grear, CEO, Promise Land Media, Inc.
Greater Diversity News & The Challenger Newspaper

"The book I credit for educating and enhancing the career seeker is WHY SHOULD I HIRE YOU? This publication enables individuals from all facets the opportunity to be imparted with a nugget of well-guarded wisdom".

Courtney A. Hammonds, President
Unique Images International

WHY SHOULD I HIRE YOU?

If you can't answer this question in
20 seconds or less,

YOU NEED THIS BOOK?

Diane
Thanks for your support
It was good seeing again
Stay in

3/24/05

Stephanie C. Harper

Table of Contents

Part 5 - Employable and Promotable

Part 6 - Paid What I Am Worth

Part 7 - Features and Benefits

Part 8- Appendix

Dedication

This book is for those who are prepared to become the creator of their work life, shaping it, instead of reacting to it.

Acknowledgements

This book would not exist without those people who pour into my life and support the vision set before me.

Thank you to my parents Celeste and Bennie for life.

Thank you to Dena Austin, for being my best friend in the whole wide word....all these years...BFI

Thank you to my Father in the Faith, Bishop Noel Jones, for teaching me how to "Read the Résumé" that will successfully help me in every area of my life.

Thank you to Pastor Toni Alvarado for teaching me how to balance the Mary and Martha in me and make time for this project.

Thank you to Apostle Johnathan Alvarado for your inspiration. Now I understand "partial obedience will never do".

Thank you to the editors: Addi Jordan, Petrina Hill and Anetra Henry for making this project a priority.
Meet you at Spondivits - my treat.

Thank you "A Time To Dance, for you for allowing me the time to prepare for YOUR future, Now get dressed, it's time get back dancing to the Glory of God!

Thank you Kimberyln R. Nelson for always taking my many calls and providing Godly input in every situation.

To my board members: Harold J. Bell, Chiquita Board, Marcellus Jackson, Velma W. Larkins, Mildred Mason, Thom Peters, Vivianne Hardy-Townes, Leutrell M. Osborne, and Josephine Williams. What on earth would I do without ya'll bossing me around? Thank you for continuing to encourage me and impart within me all your "smarts".

Thanks to Promise Land Media (Peter Great and J. Travis Reep) for being the first to publish my articles for the world to read.

Thanks to all the job seekers who made this book a necessity.

Thanks _____, go ahead and place your name here. I didn't forget about you - I just ran out of space.

Very Special Thanks

Thank you, Linda Matias, for being a leader in the "people preparation" industry and still making time to be a part of this very important project me.

Foreword

Successful career searches don't happen by accident – they are deliberate! Much of the success depends on you. It depends, quite frankly, on your determination and willingness to understand the inner workings of the search.

Working the career search can be divided into many different parts – the résumé, the search, the interview, the offer – and all parts are equally as important. Each builds upon the other. A strong résumé leads to an active career search. An active career search leads to exciting interviews. Exciting interviews lead to viable employment offers. In order for a career search to be successful, all parts must come together seamlessly.

The reality is that the career search doesn't have to be a riddle. Just like any other "relationship," the success of a job seekers courtship with a hiring organization depends on his or her drive to build an instant connection. The rules of relationship building haven't changed much. A "what's in it for me?" attitude never works. A relationship based on mutual respect and understanding always garners a positive response.

It is important – and one should add, your responsibility – to approach the career search from "the other side of the desk." That is, to properly identify the needs of a hiring organization so that you don't begin the search with blinders on. To complicate matters, the career search is also about you -- your desires, your accomplishments, and your story.

Sound confusing? That's understandable. After all, the career search has so many integral parts and your success hinges on your ability to fuse your wants and those of the hiring organization. That isn't always easy to do.

This book, WHY SHOULD I HIRE YOU? is coming at a time when job seekers are frustrated. If you are tired of distributing résumé after résumé, going on interview after interview, and yet not receiving offers, then this book has been written with you in mind.

No matter how much you think you know about the career search, this book will provide you with another perspective – THE perspective.

Linda Matias
President, CareerStrides
March 2004

Linda Matias is a recognized career expert who has been quoted a number of times in The Wall Street, New York Newsday, Newsweek and the HR-esource.com. She is President of CareerStrides (careerstides.com) and the National Résumé Writers' Association (nrwa.com).

An Invitation to become employable, promotable and get paid what you're worth.

Dear Reader,

You are about to encounter a direct connection between what to do and why it matters. The goal of this book is to share some of the principles and practices that influence hiring decisions. The theories, principals, and lessons found in this book are intended to be both educational and empowering. I have poured my passion for job seekers into this book. I offer you career seeking strategies that did not previously exist and assist you with building an employability toolbox necessary for a rewarding career. As a Fortune 500 Human Resource professional, I have had the opportunity to interview many candidates who were qualified for the position, yet unprepared for the interview, costing them great opportunities with great companies.

Career Continuation is a lifestyle for a lifetime™, purchasing this book is only the beginning. I have often said, I am amazed at how much time, energy and money people will invest in things such as weight loss, marriage counseling, fashion, credit repair, finances, stock, etc. But fail to make comparable investments into their careers. I believe your career, by extension, is your entire life. It is up to you to decide, "What it is worth to you?"

My career as a Human Resource professional has afforded me the opportunity to interview many candidates. I have seen first hand the downfalls of job seekers who are not properly prioritizing and preparing.

As a job seeker, I too did not land every position I applied for. It was frustrating because so often my skill set and the organizational need seemed to be a perfect match. Desperate for answers, I began to contact employers to ask questions. Surprisingly enough, the feedback I received was not at all what I expected. I took the feedback as constructive criticism and began to approach my career search as though I was the professional and not the job seeker.

With career advancement, my responsibilities in the human resource discipline grew. I too began to see in other job seekers, what seasoned professionals once saw in me. I began to do what

I wish all human resource professionals would do - close interviews. I did this by allowing job seekers an opportunity to talk about the interview process. Job seekers were not only grateful, but began to inquire about résumé tips, interview strategies and other career planning options. Referrals became clients, and soon I had a part-time position preparing job seekers. As clients grew so did my desire to assist job seekers in the area of preparation.

I have written this book to share invaluable information with job seekers whom I could not personally reach or may never come in contact with.   I thank you for supporting this publication. Hopefully, it will give you what you need to obtain your career goals. Remember... Excellence is not what you do - it's who you are.™   Choose to excel today! May all of your career endeavors be established, strengthened, perfected and settled.

Happy Reading,

Stephanie C. Harper, PHR, CCP, CHRM
President, P.H.D. Career Strategies
Author, Career Expert and Speaker
Your career planning and development specialist

A few words of clarification for the purpose of this book!

Job Seeker

Anyone who is unemployed, underemployed, unhappily employed or not being paid what they are worth.

Human Resource Professional

A certified professional in the field of human resources who possess the proven skill, knowledge, and ability to align organizational goals with human assets.

Hiring Manager

The non-human resource professional tasked with interviewing and other hiring activity.

Part 1
Establish

Section 1
Why Should I Hire You?

Section 2
I Understand Your Position

Section 3
Completing the Employability Toolbox

Section 4
Why Do I Need All of This?

Why Should I Hire You?

Section 1
WHY SHOULD I HIRE YOU?™

Think back to your last interview, where you asked any of the following questions?

- Tell me about yourself?
- What are your qualifications?
- Why Should I Hire You?

These are normal interview questions. A job seeker who plans to become employed can not offer normal responses. A serious job seeker has read one or more "how to" books about becoming and remaining gainfully employed. In this competitive environment, you cannot afford to give cookie-cutter responses that are suggested in some career related books such as: hardworking, dependable, a team player, result oriented and a fast learner. While those are great examples of action words; they are not answers to the any of the three questions posed. The truth of the matter is they do not tell the interviewer anything about you.

Why? They provide no supporting evidence to be believable and viable examples of who you are or what you can contribute to the organization.

Why? 9 out of 10 applicants applying for the same position will give the same answers or answers very similar.

Why? It is important for job seekers to find unique and creative ways to gain the attention of prospective employers.

Why? Job Seekers need to approach their job search with the attitude of "I'm not competing for this company, this company is competing for me". However, before you can compete, you must be complete. Employers are taking necessary steps to ensure that the right person is hired into an organization. When an employer asks interview questions, they are not just going through the motions. They are trying to get down to the bottom line, which is "WHY SHOULD I HIRE YOU?"

The question human resource professional ask and what they really want to know are not always the same. In this book, you will be able to assess and build your employability toolbox. In today's tough employment market, it is not enough to just arm yourself with a cover letter and a résumé.

Ask yourself, if I were sitting on the other side of the desk, "WOULD I HIRE ME?" If your response was yes, based on any of the following:

- I need a job
- I have bills to pay or
- I heard you were hiring

Unfortunately, you are not ready to compete. The good news is you are doing something about it.

Section 2

I understand your position!

HR MANAGEMENT

Job Analysis
Recruitment and
Selection
Compensation
Health & Safety
Strategic Planning

HR Planning
Training / Development
Benefit Administration
Employee Relations
Globalization

Job Seeker

Position - employment for which one has been hired.

People have often inquired "why is it so hard to get into human resources?" It is not as difficult as most think. However, to understand human resources fully, it is best to start on the ground floor. The many disciplines of human resource management can be more complex than you can imagine. For the job seeker, understanding human resource management is a vital part of becoming and remaining gainfully employed.

The purpose of this book is to help job seekers adopt the mindset of the human resource professional. Before you can adopt the mindset of a human resource professional, you must first understand human resource management. The average job seeker may not have a realistic view of "a day in the life" of a human resource professional. We will explore the many disciplines of human resources management to educate job seekers and help them to conduct their job search from the human resource perspective. After all, this is the perception that determines if you will or will not be chosen to interview with a prospective employer. Simply put, get ready to understand

7

what the professional knows and looks for when selecting the best candidate.

While there is no typical day in human resources, thus creating a love for the profession, most human resource professionals work 12-hour days, have endless meetings and answer more than 100 emails per day (both internal and external) and still manage to smile at the end of the day. For the Human Resource professional it is never about us - it is about what is best for the company.

What is Human Resource Management?

Human Resource Management (HRM) is the effective management of people at work. HRM examines what can or should be done to make working people more productive and satisfied.

What is the function of Human Resource Management?

Human Resource Management is the function performed in organizations that facilitates the most effective use of people (employees) to achieve organizational and individual goals.

Human Resource Management involves playing a major role in ensuring an organization will survive and prosper. People limit or enhance strengths and weaknesses of an organization. Effective human resource management is *building* and *protecting* the most valuable asset of any enterprise - people!

How is Human Resource Management measured?

It should be pointed out that a significant reason for the eventful success of any human resource management activity is the organization's employees are the best qualified and are performing tasks or functions that suit their needs, skills and abilities.

So forget the negative perception that you previously had about human resource professionals up this point (perfectionist, tyrant, enforcer, unfair, bossy, etc). Hopefully, you are gaining a better understanding of how and why human resource professionals operate in the manner they do and why the functions they provide must be effective. The human resource professional is hired to effectively manage people, which is an impossible task in itself. When an organization is operating in chaos, the human resource professional is not effectively operating in its required function.

The human resource professional sadly understands that a portion of our paycheck dictates, "employees are not going to always like you or the rules you make". However, the larger portion of our paycheck dictates that we are to "align our employees with the overall goal of the organization to ensure we are operating effectively". Just as a job seeker must take part in career planning, human resource professionals must take part in human resource planning, which are both a process and a set of plans.

When seeking to fill a position, human resource management involves maintaining a skills inventory of the current staff among many other things. By keeping track of this, human resources professionals are better able to forecast if the opening will be filled through an internal or external candidate and expedite the time to fill. Successful human resource management starts with having a successful pool of candidates to pull from.

This is where the focus turns to the job seeker. Job Seekers can be internal, external candidates or both. To the hiring manager, it doesn't matter as long as it is THE BEST CANDIDATE. There are pro's and con's to consider during this process.

HUMAN RESOURCES

INTERNAL
CANDIDATE

EXTERNAL
CANDIDATE

Internal

- **Pro's**
- Acclimated to the company culture.
- Has established relationships.
- Proven work ethics.

- **Con's**
- Leaves vacancy in the department/company.
- Previous work habits or ethics can work against you.
- Possibility of having to supervise "friends".

External
- **Pro's**
- Varied skills, knowledge and experience.
- Offers a fresh outlook, which is unbiased.
- "Under new management" - changes can be made.

- **Con's**
- Changes make you look like the bad guy.
- No relationship with the decision makers.
- Unsure of the company's expectations.

A job seeker can be saved from "heart burn" by understanding why the functions of human resource management are in place and why structuring the career search around these functions has a direct impact on the success of the company.

Preview the following chart for clarity on influences, acquiring, rewarding, developing, maintaining and the desired results of human resource management and began to see how human resource professionals must match your qualifications to ensure productivity and profit.

DOMESTIC MODEL FOR HUMAN RESOURCE MANAGEMENT
(DIAGNOSE, PRESCRIBE, IMPLEMENT, EVALUATE)

EXTERNAL INFLUENCES

- Government requirements, regulations and laws
- Unions
- Economic Conditions
- Competitiveness
- Composition of labor force
- Location of organization

INTERNAL INFLUENCES

- Strategy
- Goals
- Organizational culture
- Nature of the task
- Work group
- Leader's style and experience

(Concerned about people and results)

AQUIRING HUMAN RESOURCES

- Equal Employment Opportunity
- HR Planning
- Job Analysis and Design
- Recruitment and Assimilation
- Selection

REWARDING HUMAN RESOURCES

- Performance Evaluation
- Compensation
- Job Analysis and Design
- Benefits and Services

(FOCUS ON EACH PROCESS IS ON PEOPLE AND RESULTS)

DEVELOPING HUMAN RESOURCES

- Training and Development
- Career Planning
- Discipline

MAINTAINING AND PROTECTING HUMAN RESOURCES

- Labor Relations
- Collective Bargaining
- Safety, health, and wellness
- Evaluation

DESIRED END RESULTS
Socially responsible and ethical practices, competitive, high quality products and services

- Labor Relations
- Collective Bargaining
- Safety, health, and wellness
- Evaluation

11

Job Analysis

As a job seeker, have you even considered all of these steps to be part of the hiring process? There are more steps, as we will discover later in the recruiting process. Consider the difference between success and failure of the organization is how well the employees perform their tasks. Therefore before considering a new hire, the decision maker has to create the ideal candidate to complete the task. The ideal candidate is developed through a process called "job analysis.

Job Analysis provides answers to questions such as these:

- How much time does it takes to complete important tasks?

- What tasks are grouped together and considered a job?

- How is a job designed to enhance employee performance?

- What kind of behavior is needed to perform the job?

- What kind of person (traits/experience) is best suited for the job?

STEPS IN THE JOB ANALYSIS PROCESS (1-6)

Step 1	Examine the organization and fit of each job.
Step 2	Determine how job analysis information will be
Step 3	used.
Step 4	Select jobs to be analyzed.
Step 5	Collect data by using job analysis techniques.
Step 6	Prepare job descriptions.
	Prepare job specs.

Use information for Steps 1- 6 for:

Job Design
Planning
Recruitment
Selection and Training
Performance Evaluation
Compensation and Benefits
EEO Compliance
Follow-up Evaluations

The decision maker has already determined the ideal candidate. It is essential that you have the confidence to convey that you are the ideal candidate. You have to convince the interviewer that they have created the position, **just for you**. **But before you can compete, you must be COMPLETE!**

Why Should I Hire You?

Section 3

Completing the Employability Toolbox

All Candidates Look Alike

WHY YOU MUST BE DIFFERENT

Tool - something (instrument of apparatus) used in performing an operation necessary in the practice of a vocation or profession.

Believe it or not on paper, all candidates look alike. Many job seekers will set expectations (pay, environment, industry, etc.) for an employer, but rarely hold themselves to the same expectations. As a job seeker, you must have the appropriate tools to set yourself apart. An employer is not obligated to employ you simply because you need to work. The challenge of the human resource professional to align human assets with organizational goals requires training.

We learned in the previous chapter, there are many employment laws and practices to contend with; personalities to match, organizations to build, day-to-day operations to go

15

forth and it is up to the human resource professional to make it happen. Employers are seeking the individual with the most complete package; let's call this the employability toolbox.

Employability - capable of being employed

Toolbox - a chest for tools

There are many contents, which complete an employability toolbox. Other factors will determine if you are the right person for the position. This includes being employable, promotable and being paid what you are worth. One thing to note is 3% of job seekers are not employable. It may take several steps on your part *before* you are employable and it certainly takes time, energy and investment.

Unfortunately, the challenge is few job seekers posses an employability toolbox - this should be an exception and not the rule. Sure, you have a résumé and cover letter, everyone does, however; the résumé and cover letter alone are not an employability toolbox. The difference in becoming and remaining gainfully employed is how you start the interview process.

Human resource professionals are trained to spot the difference between utilizing cookie-cutters (fill in the blank) and utilizing professional services. Professionally prepared cover letters and résumés are hard to come by. Don't forget, for the human resource professional, this is an area of expertise. In fact, most human resource professional have seen enough résumés during their careers to know a cookie cutter at a glance. Opinions are formed about you and your work ethics based on the quality of your presentation. The average résumé only has a 7-second preview (initially), and you never know the skill level of the person reviewing the résumé.

Sadly enough, to some reading a résumé is like reading a credit report - often misinterpreted. Résumé reading is an internal on-the-job skill learned. Just as an engineer learns to read blue prints, the human resource professional learns to read a résumé. This is to the benefit of the job seeker because you may have the opportunity to market yourself during the face-to-face interview.   While we have touched briefly on the résumé and cover letter, let's closely examine all of the contents of the employability toolbox and their function.

THE CONTENTS OF AN EMPLOYABILITY TOOLBOX
(not necessarily in this order)

Career Personality Assessment
(Dreams to details)

Cover Letter
(Identify your target)

Résumé
(Eliminate the competition)

Resu-Cards™
(Networking)

Compensation Overview
(Know your value)

Interview Techniques
(Impact people)

Career Planning
(Secure the foundation)

Career Development and Progression Plan
(Continued Education and Training)

Why Should I Hire You?

Section 4

WHY DO I NEED ALL OF THIS -

WHAT PURPOSE DOES THIS SERVE?

**Purpose - something set up as an object or
end to be attained.**

Cover Letter

A cover letter serves two purposes:

1) to introduce yourself to the potential employer

2) to see if you (the job seeker) follows directions, ie: including salary history, fax résumé, no phone calls, only candidates with relevant experience will be considered, etc.)

A cover letter is always necessary when seeking employment, especially when the employer asks for information such as salary history or references. Remember the K.I.S.S. rule (keep it short and simple). Use your cover letter for its intended purpose and do not simply duplicate your résumé.

Imagine a human resource professional with 150 -200 résumés on their desk. One (1) opening with a two (2) days to fill the position. The résumé to be eliminated will be the one that requires the most reading. Considering that you have a 2-page résumé - adding the cover letter places you at 3 pages. If it takes 3 pages or more, to prove that you are the right candidate, you may not be considered at all. Primarily because there are only 2-days to fill the position. There is simply not enough time to read all of your information. In some cases, less is more. Pique the interest of your prospective employer, but do not tell the whole story. After all, if you tell the whole story on paper, what is left to warrant an interview?

Being able to effectively (produce an effect) and efficiently (with minimal waste) prepare your credentials requires skill of a seasoned professional who understand the industry and knows what a human resource professional is looking for. If you are not an expert in this field, stick to that you know and let the expert produce a reader-friendly résumé to obtain the desired results.

Here a few tips to remember:

✓ Format your contact information identical to the contact information on your résumé.

✓ State your position interest in the first 2 lines of the cover letter.

✓ Only Include direct accomplishments, which are relevant to the position listing.

✓ Make sure the cover letter is brief, but complete.

✓ Do not list any personal information or extra curricular items.

✓ Only list salary expectations and references when requested in the job posting.

✓ Reference job titled when supplied

The closer the information resembles the position description - the more you look like the ideal candidate.

SAMPLE REQUISITION

REQ NUMBER

Position: Job Seeker
Start Date: Immediate

Requirements:

Seeking serious job seeker

Seeking promotable person

Candidate who follows direction.

Only applicants with valid contact phone will be considered

Mail Cover Letter and Resume to:
P.H.D. Career Strategies
Attention: Human Resource Manager
P.O. Box 54166
Atlanta, GA 30308

EXAMPLE
Job Seeker

123 Main Street, Anywhere, USA 1111 ▪ 404-555-1212 ▪ mail @.com

August 15, 2003

P.H.D. Career Strategies
Attention: Human Resource Manager
P.O. Box 54166
Atlanta, GA 30308

RE: JOB SEEKER POSITION - POSTING #123

Dear Prospective Employer:

With interest, <u>I am applying for the position of Job Seeker</u>. By way of this letter allow me to introduce myself, and share why I am the best candidate for the position.

Your Requirements	My Qualifications
Seeking a serious job seeker	I have made an investment to complete my employability toolbox.
Candidate who follows instructions	I have included a cover letter answering on the questions asked.
Seeking a promotable person	I have current skills that are transferable for other positions.

Based on the above information, I am confident that your organizational need and my skill set are a perfect match. I am available to interview and commence employment immediately. I can be reached at 404-555-1212.

Best regards,
Job Seeker

P.S. Salary request are part of the selection process. An allotted pay range is preset and may qualify or disqualify you based on the criteria.

Résumé

A resume is not intended to get you a position, but to grant you an interview. The résumé is the beginning of the interview process. The first impression a prospective employer will have of you is based on the quality of your résumé or lack of. Often first impressions are not favorable, due to grammatical errors, typos, misspelled words and incorrect contact information and the overall appearance of the résumé. All of which give the employer the right to assume this with match the quality of your work. The résumé is your first impression and shows the employer exactly how you present yourself to others.

The human resource professional is looking for more than your qualifications. They are also looking to see if you are an organizational fit (employable), promotable and paid what you are worth. If you are not taking pride in how you present yourself, how well with you represent the company? A large part of your presentation is how well you can present yourself on paper.

If an employer finds it hard read your résumé, due to the size of the font being too small. There is a chance the employer will not attempt to do so. If your résumé has contact information crossed out and hand-written, there is a chance the employer may not view you as a professional. If you use colored paper, and it is considered to be design or flyer paper as opposed to résumé paper, you may stand out, but for the wrong reason. If your résumé has too many designs or logo's, it may not be a scannable document that an employer can use.

Take the time to consider the presentation of your current resume. If you were the one to receive your résumé what would your honest first impression be?

EXAMPLE

Job Seeker

123 Main Street, Anywhere, USA 11111■
404-555-1212 ▪ mail@msn.com

SUMMARY
Compete Employability Toolbox
I understand what I'm worth
Promotable with Transferable Skills
Available to commence employment immediately

EDUCATION
Employability Training, P.H.D. Career Strategies University
Atlanta, GA 2003

EXPERIENCE
List only 10 years of work experience
Show a complete time frame for employment tenures
Identify accomplishments
Do not use the companies' reputation to build yourself
Provide computer programs knowledge – not a list
List experience only relevant to the position you are seeking

PROFESSIONAL AFFILIATIONS
List items that are only career related and current
Do not list personal information or items to draw prejudice

REFERENCES
Use this space to market yourself, an employer will ask for them.

Before we continue with the remaining employability toolbox contents. Let's pause here and talk a bit more about cover letters and résumés. Now that we are familiar with the function of each, I would like to pose a question. If everyone knows what cover letters and résumés are, why are common mistakes not so common when it comes to job seekers?

Below we'll cover some job seeking mistakes that will guarantee a résumé makes it to FILE 13 (trash):

- Not utilizing a professional to prepare a cover letter or résumé.

It is not a wise career decision to have someone who does not understand your career goal, prepare your credentials.

Why? They have no idea what a trained professional is looking for. There is more to the résumé than the format. While a great format is key, the content is just as important.

- Not making the necessary investment for the best presentation possible.

Making an investment in your career is well worth the expense. Be sure the person preparing the résumé has real world experience and proven ability to write a winning cover letter or résumé. Make sure they have proven skills that have been obtained by working in a human resource environment. Be careful of people who have resource functions, but do not actually work in a human resource environment. While their areas of expertise in recruiting, training, benefit administration, etc, is invaluable. There is a difference between a human resource professional and a person who handles some human resource functions. It is to your benefit to find people who understand the full cycle of human resources as opposed to only specializing in one area of the trade.

- Relying on Internet résumé templates or fill in the blank software.

These templates are designed for a quick fix, a simple fill in the blank module. They are intended to be a guide . You cannot "simply" fill in the blank and expect to look any different than the next candidate.

- Utilizing word processors for résumé writers.

Be very careful when selecting an agency or service to prepare your cover letter and résumé. Housewives, administrative professionals and graphic artist have capitalized on document preparation.

For a job seeker, you need career preparation. Most résumé writing services will charge a minimum of anywhere from $150 to $200 or more for a professionally prepared résumé, but don't get bend out of shape. Remember you are not paying for the pages; you are paying for the expertise that will be transferred to the page. Don't just look at the price, consider the final outcome will increase your chance of landing the position you desire.

- Using Copy Centers

Most copy centers that offer these services use Graphic Designers who are of course not human resource professionals nor professional résumé writers. This is not beneficial to you as a job seeker. In fact, this it is a disservice - the time you spend waiting is time you could spend career searching.

No matter what route you choose, you will make some type of impression. Be certain that it is your best. You never get a second chance to make a first impression. To ensure your résumé passes the 7-second rule, job seekers need to be able to create visibility, creditability, and creativity.
- **Visibility - the capability of being easily observed.**

- **Creditability – worthy of belief.**

- **Creativity– characterized by originality and expressiveness.**

A human resource professional spending a minimum of 3 years or more in the career field has seen more than their share of résumés. The good, bad and the unmentionable! It only takes a quick scan to tell the difference between the most qualified candidates based on the required criteria for the position and the résumé that belongs in file 13 - trash.

Ensuring your résumé does not end up in file 13 is determined by knowing not only the position you are seeking, but also knowing the company that you expect to employ you. The people hired can become a direct reflection of the human resource professionals' ability to be effective in what they were hired to do. For the job seeker, this is a critical part of the interview process. The fastest way to be eliminated from the pile is to look like the other candidates.

Even though many corporations now scan résumés into a database, being chosen for the interview depends on how your résumé is prepared. The technology of scanning résumés is intended to simplify the recruiting process. It can however make it difficult for job seekers to match criteria. In many larger companies were résumés are being scanned into a database there is a tendency to misplace candidates and incorrectly classify them. For example, if you are an Office Manager who has also been tasked with bookkeeping as part of your responsibilities, it is possible that you can be classified as an accounting professional. Therefore receiving calls for accounting positions that you are not qualified for.

Why? The computer has located buzzwords such as accounts payable and receivable and has possibly classified you as both and administrator and an accountant. While this can simplify the intake process, it can complicate the hiring process.

If you are clearly indicating that you are seeking a position of Office Manager, yet receiving calls such as this, your résumé has been scanned. Technology has replaced the traditional way of seeking employment and many job seekers are relying on technology to introduce themselves to potential employers. Your objective here is NOT to get stuck on the information highway.

According to a study by Drake Beam Morin, only 6% of hires at the management level currently occur through any Internet site

27

as opposed to 61%, which occur through networking. A separate study conducted by Spherion showed only 7% of positions were obtained through an Internet board.

Only
6%-7%

While I strongly advocate using job boards to showcase your skills to employers (it is also a creative way to let your résumé work for you), I also believe that technology has provided effortless, yet instant avenues to arrive at the company's door. Your objective as a job seeker is not to simply arrive, but to be inviting inside, asked to sit down and stay a while. The outcome is up to you. Once you are inside, you still have work to do to stay inside. On today's information highway, it is easy for your résumé to end up in a cluttered database and your odds of being selected for a position equal winning the lottery.

If your objective is to GET HIRED!™, you have to do more than "pick a format" and hit submit to get your credentials in the hands of the decision maker. You have to do something that ensures you stand out in the stack. Don't forget you will need one résumé for face-to-face interviews and one résumé for the Internet. When applying for specific positions, be sure your résumé projects identifiable criteria. A résumé has **3 areas of easily identifiable criteria** to be considered for a position.

- **Relevant Experience (tenure in the field)**
- **Relevant Education (written instruction)**
- **Relevant Knowledge (make it happen)**

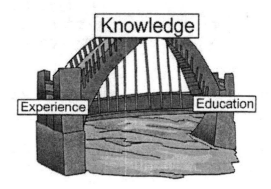

You will note many employers will ask for a degree. But most employers want experience. <u>Knowledge</u> of the position is the bridge between your <u>experience</u> and your <u>education</u>. How you convey these criteria in your cover letter and résumé are what make you visible.

When using the information highway a few house-keeping rules apply when you are sending your credentials through email. According to Eliston Word Processing Plus her are some guidelines for writing an effective email:

An effective email:

- Is brief, yet grabs the reader's attention.

- Provides information, makes a recommendation, or asks for action.

- Supports your position or explains benefits to the reader.

- Gives reader a call to action and mentions the next steps or deadlines.

Always use the four-step approach to writing:

- Plan what you want to say.

- Write a draft.

- Revise the draft.

- Edit.

Other rules to keep in mind:

- Email is not completely secure. Choose your words carefully; your email can easily be forwarded to others.

- Email is not considered proper for "official business" (always follow - up by sending a hard copy of your résumé and/or a phone call).

- Keep to one subject per email.

- Avoid using all uppercase or lowercase - upper case is considered yelling.

- Avoid using fancy formatting such as: fonts, bold, underline, italics, etc.

- Realize that humor and emotions can be lost or misinterpreted.

- Avoid uploading long or numerous attachments unless you have permission to do so.

- When replying to emails exclude the original message. Only send enough of the message to refresh the recipient's memory.

- When sending large groups, use the BCC field to protect the privacy and email addresses or others in the group.

- Use a signature or file line to identify yourself and provide alternative ways to be contacted.

Part 2
Strengthen

Section 5
I Am Visible and I Stand Out in the Stack

Section 6
Interview Strategies

Section 7
I Know What You Are Thinking

Section 8
The Best "Me" on the Planet

Why Should I Hire You?

Section 5

"I'm visible and I stand out in the stack"

Visible - devised to keep a particular part or item always in full view or readily seen or referred to.

It does not matter if you are an Engineer, Office Manger, Accountant, Teacher, Administrative Assistant, Bookkeeper, or Truck Driver. On paper all candidates look alike. They each have a name, address, phone number, objective, and list of job titles, duties and dates. Most are on white paper with black ink. Let me pause here and say - please do not use colored ink on your résumé, unless your profession requires it - such as a Graphic Artist.

What you do as a job seeker to gain the attention of the decision maker is what makes the difference in how long you remain a job seeker. Here is the reality behind the process, you want the employer to take notice of you, but gaining the right attention is key. You are going to have to prove that you are the best person for the position. You don't want to put yourself in a place, where the hiring manager has to question your judgment long before reviewing your credentials. Before you are granted an interview, you have to first stand out in the stack.

A human resource manager or hiring manager can review 100 or more résumés before choosing one (1) good candidate to conduct a simple phone interview. Finding ten qualified candidates can be a difficult task to accomplish when there is a pile of résumés that look alike. Take a 3 second glance at the following three résumés and find the similarities. To prove the point, remember you only have 3 seconds then you must look away.

Candidate #1

> Jane Smith
> 101 Tulip Road,
> Atlanta, GA 30308
> 404-555-1212
>
> - Filing
> - Faxing
> - Answering Phones

Candidate # 2

> Paula Prince
> 522 West Circle Way
> Atlanta, GA 30308
> 404-555-1213
>
> - Filing
> - Faxing
> - Answering Phones

Candidate #3

> Jane Smith
> 101 Tulip Road,
> Atlanta, GA 30308
> 404-555-1212
>
> - Filing
> - Faxing
> - Answering Phones

At first glance did you notice that Candidates #1 and #3 were the same candidate who happen to look different? If so, great! While Paula and Phyllis are both administrative professionals who file, fax and answer phones. Phyllis appears to be a more polished professional with career progression.

The objective here was to show you how much time is spent reviewing a résumé at first glance. Imagine this same exercise with a full-page résumé in a stack of 200 résumés. While résumés 1 and 3 are the exact same résumé. The paper alone will make candidate #3 stand out in the stack. Another important factor to consider is the human resource professional looks at paper continuously during the day in various forms, emails, reports, applications, etc. It is just refreshing to see something that looks different. Can you make a lasting impression in just 7 seconds? Certainly, with the right tools!

Another area to consider is the wording you choose for your résumé - also known as buzzwords. For the sake of illustration and clarity, we will continue to use an administrative résumé. Imagine having to preview 50 resumes in the same profession. All will list, filing, faxing and answering phones. But the one that stands out will be the résumé, which gives the employer a clear range of skill level or professionalism; the one who lists accomplishments as opposed to routine duties. In a profession of having to view résumés all day every day, one that stands out with accomplishments is an easy ready and makes the decision maker want to read it.

Let's take a look at two sample candidate résumés of administrative professionals who do the same work, yet one has mastered the art of expanded word communication.

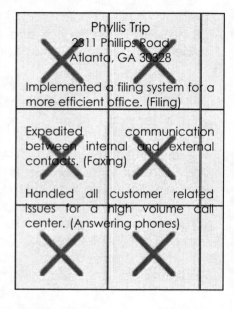

Paula Prince	Phyllis Trip
522 West Circle Atlanta, GA 30318 404-555-1212	~~2311 Phillips Road~~ ~~Atlanta, GA 30328~~
• Filing • Faxing • Answering Phones	Implemented a filing system for a more efficient office. (Filing) Expedited communication between internal and external contacts. (Faxing) Handled all customer related issues for a high volume call center. (Answering phones)

At first glance, many human resource professionals or hiring managers can tell just how much time or money you have - or have not - invested in your preparation. It is necessary to have clean, crisp copies of everything. In some instances assistants and administrators who are not yet professionals in the filed are the first to process and preview incoming résumés.

For this person, their position can involve a lot of paper pushing and become monotonous. This process is similar to the process used by large corporations to scan résumés. The difficulty is, neither the inexperienced professional nor the computers are trained to catch red flags. This is not something that is taught, but rather learned with growth in the human resource profession. Unfortunately, what is underlined below is all they will see on your résumé as this is what they are trained to look for.

SAMPLE REQUISTION

Certification
5 years of experience
College Degree
Manufacturing
Word
Excel
PowerPoint.

MATCHING RESUME

Summary
A certified administrative
professional with 5 years
of experience

Work Experience
Administrative Assistant
to Manufacturing
Manager, proficient with
Microsoft Suite.

Education
B.S. Administration,
1992

Whatever you do, be sure that you are the one who stands out in the pile. Here are few inexpensive, yet creative ways to submit your résumé and ensure that you will stand out in the stack.

- Hire a professional résumé writer who is able to clearly produce a winning résumé

- Be sure to use acceptable Colored Paper

- Using colored paper is not enough. You must use high quality résumé (linen) paper.

- Custom Formats (Digital Resume on CD) Resu-disk™

37

A résumé on CD is not as expensive or complicated as you think. But it does provide you with a sure way to stand out in the stack! Most employers will preview it just out of curiosity. Coupled with your resu-card™ an employer will certainly take notice of you. This too, needs to be professionally prepared to capture your target audience and to be effective (producing desired results).

Using a resu-disk™, must be efficient and effective to the receiver and it should be formatted so that it is user friendly. This is a new, yet inexpensive, innovative concept that is sure to impress an employer and show up other job seekers. Your résu-disk™ alone, may spark up a marketing ideas for the company and now you have just become a "necessary resource". A job seeker must pull out all stops to ensure there is power in presence.

Power - the ability to act or produce an effect
Presence - a quality of poise and effectiveness that enables a performer to achieve a close relationship with their audience.

In short...as a job seeker, you must be able to come into relationship with your audience (decision makers) and be able to produce an effect. You will accomplish this by completing your employability toolbox and knocking the socks of your prospective employer. Making the investment in your job search tells the decision maker that you are serious about your career. Finding creative avenues gives a prospective employer a glimpse at who you are and what you will bring to the table. Remember the objective is not only to become employable, but also to be promotable and get paid what you are worth.

Career Personality Assessment (CPA)

CPA's are designed to help you understand why it is important for your personality type and career choice line up.

Career - a field for or pursuit of consecutive "progressive" achievement. (A job is defined by Webster's collegiate dictionary as "to do odd or occasional pieces of work).

Personality - the characteristic way a person thinks and behaves in adjusting to an environment (includes a persons traits, values, motives, genetic blueprint, attitudes, emotional reactivity, abilities, self-image, and intelligence)

Assessment -to determine the size, value of importance of.

Your desire to make the difference between a job and a career for yourself will determine your priorities and how much time, planning and investment you place in your career search.

Success to most people is summed up as "who other people think you are" But I believe that a career is not who you are, but what you do! Case and point, I am a sister, daughter, aunt and a friend. My profession is Career Planning, Development, and Human Resources. A personality assessment is important if you want a career that you will enjoy. Sure you can excel in any career with hard work, but why not pursue a career that will provide you with both professional and personal fulfillment?

Powerful emotional forces motivate people, and work provides an opportunity for the expression of both aggressive and pleasure-seeking drives. Understanding your personality type will help to differentiate attitude from preference.

Attitude - a characteristic and usually long-lasting way of thinking, feeling and behaving.

Preference - a type of attitude that evaluates in a positive or negative way.

EXAMPLE
My personality type is an Extrovert, extremely outgoing with a keen sense of evaluating effectiveness. My Personality test suggests that I would enjoy work in counseling, law, human resource management or educational administration.

Here are the characteristics of an extrovert.
- talkative, likes to talk, sometimes without thinking
- develop many interest
- like to get involved, make things happen
- notice the whole picture
- theoretical - interested in "why" it works
- creative, like to experiment
- appreciate sensitivity
- quick to offer support
- merciful - individual circumstances noted
- comfortable when things are organized
- like to have a time framed schedule
- decides quickly, but accurately
- methodical - make a plan, use it!

After spending over 14 years in the "people environment" and still enjoying the work I do, I would say that this is an accurate match between my personality type and my career choice. Certainly I have excelled in other areas such as serving as an artistic director, singing, creating things, teaching and the like, but all of these professions involve managing human resources or people.

Surely, I would have loved to take a CPA years ago before testing the waters in other areas of responsibility such as accounting. While I have the ability to do accounting functions, this is not an area that I would enjoy doing for a living. My accounting responsibilities have proved to be beneficial as those same skills have since become transferable for other things. For some personality types accounting is a career match, but for me, it was not a CAREER CHOICE.

Resu-Cards™

Resu-Cards™ are intended to produce your qualifications when you cannot provide a résumé on the spot.

A study by Spherion showed 12% of people have obtained offers of employment through a business card. Which proves job seekers need cards too. It is an invaluable networking tool that you can take with your everywhere. As a job seeker, you should make it a practice to always enter a public setting with a resu-card™. Career opportunities are everywhere; you may meet your next employer standing in line at the grocery store, movie counter, bowling alley, fitness center, or even at the bus stop. There are many usable resu-cards™ formats. The best format will mirror and highlight the accomplishments on your résumé.

Would you take an employer seriously if they ripped a corner from a sheet of paper and said "call me about employment opportunities". Probably not! As a job seeker, why would an employer take you seriously if you did the same thing? Not only will your resu-card™ impress your potential employer, it is also a great conversation piece and shows that you are concerned about your presentation.

Job Seeking should be considered a full-time job and you are not successful at it until you are hired. Be careful not to list goals on your resu-card™. This is the time to list accomplishments that you can back up.

Stephanie C. Harper
404.299.8757

President and CEO of P.H.D. Career Strategies

Career Columnist of the P.H.D. Perspective contributing articles to The Challenger Newspaper, Greater Diversity and Onyx Woman Magazine

Author Best Selling Career Book
WHY SHOULD I HIRE YOU?

Section 6
Interview Strategies

Interview - a formal consultation to evaluate qualifications.

Strategies - a careful plan or method.

The purpose of the interview is to check you out. Many résumés are fabricated, usually in the areas of titles, tenure, and salary (when included). Employers verify your credentials using the interview process to check you out. Ever wonder what an employer may need to check out during the process that they could not check out by just reading your cover letter and résumé?

Some are checking for your appearance:

- the way you look
  (includes hair styles, make-up, finger nails, attire, etc.)
- the way you behave
- the way you write
- the way you speak

40% of job seekers who stay unemployed do so because their appearance does not match up to the employers' expectations.

Others are checking to see if you fit into the company culture:

- -can you represent the company and its image
- -can you be presented to clients
- -can you be presented to vendors, etc.
- -can you be presented to other employees

Most are checking to see if you measure up to your credentials.

- Knowledge
- Skill
- Ability

During the interview, remember these three major elements of presentation:

The opener
"tell what you are going to tell"
The body
"where you actually tell them"
The close
"tell them what you just told them"

In the introduction of the book, we listed examples of action words such as hardworking, dependable, a team player, result-oriented and a fast learner. But imagine how much more effective your presentation would be if you responded differently than all the other job seekers.

EXAMPLE

Interviewer:
WHY SHOULD I HIRE YOU?™

Candidate #1:
I'm Hardworking, dependable, a team player, result-oriented, and a fast learner. (basically says "train me!)

Interviewer:
WHY SHOULD I HIRE YOU?™

Candidate 2:
I am a certified job seeker with 15 years of multi industry experience in the areas of job preparation, networking and career planning. I have the education and hands on experience required to perform this position. I am promotable and confident that your organizational need and my skill set are a perfect match. (Exudes confidence and challenges the employer to compete for you).

This response will floor the interviewer. Not only was the response of candidate #2 impressive, but it also gave the interviewer the following information.

I am a certified <hardworker> job seeker with 15 years <proven knowledge in the field> of multi industry experience in the areas of job preparation, networking and career planning <where the experience is>. I possess the education <achiever> and hands on experience <on the job training> required to perform this position. I am promotable <not a job hopper> and confident that your organizational need and my skill set are a perfect match <positive outlook>.

An interview is 62% body language, 28% tone of voice and only 10% words. Make every word count - especially the questions you ask!

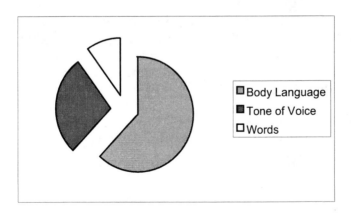

Body Language
Tone of Voice
Words

Before the interview, research the company and be prepared to give specific examples of where and how you fit into the company structure. An interview is the perfect time for a job seeker to check out a company and be prepared to interview the interviewer of the company. The time you spend interviewing the company is as equally important as the time you spend preparing for your career.

After all this is potentially the place you will be required to show up everyday. Because there are more candidates than openings, the interviewer goes into the interview looking for weaknesses and every reason to eliminate you. It is almost impossible to qualify before disqualifying. With so many candidates, a line must be drawn somewhere.

While, you may find commonalities (alumni, industry contacts, background, training, ethnicity, sororities, fraternities, mutual colleagues, etc.) between yourself and the interviewer, remain professional and resist the temptation to become personal - at all cost. Many job seekers loose out on the interview because they become more personal and less professional during the interview. This may sound harsh, but interviewing is based on an effective business decision - not a personal decision or community allegiance.

Ever had a wonderful interview in which you and the interviewer talked about everything but your credentials or your ability to perform? You were sure that you had the position, yet wondered why they never called to hire you. They knew nothing about your work habits after you left - the end result, it was not a good interview.

To show interest in the employer and the position, always prepare to ask at least three questions during your interview. Here are a few to consider:

1. Why is this position available?

It forces the employer to tell you more about the position than just what the written description portrays and given insight on the company structure.

2. Why do you enjoy working here or how long have you been employed with this company?

It forces the employer to "let their hair down". Just as employers are trained in behavioral interviewing, here is a quick course for the job seeker. If the interviewer has a sudden change in demeanor, they may also be looking for something new. If the interviewer shows excitement, it is sign of a great company or a person who really enjoys their work - but most people will be very honest when this question is asked, especially when they are caught off guard.

3. What will be expected of me in the first six (6) months to one (1) year?

This is a tricky question. Listen carefully for the answer. Realistically, the timeframe indicated should be allotted for you to become the best you can be in the _current position_ you are interviewing for. The first year in a position is not the time to seek raises or promotions but to ensure that you are aligning yourself with the organizational goals. While, it does happen, it is rare for a person to be promoted or transferred in as little as 6 months.

Be careful not to make the mistake of seeking a professional résumé writer to prepare your credentials and not be able to effectively articulate _everything_ on your résumé. A professional résumé writer will provide you with direction on career planning or refer you to an agency that can help you compliment your new cover letter and résumé ensuring you get the best use of your investment. Human Resources is human resources no matter what industry the professional works in. You never know what industry the person interviewing you has worked in, so your résumé must reflect an accurate picture of your career history and you are the product being marketed - be prepared to sell yourself!

Section 7
I know what you're thinking?

Think - to use the powers of the mind, as in conceiving ideas, drawing inferences and making judgements.

The expression "it's not what you say, but how you say it" is vital in during the interview process. As we learned in the previous chapter, non-verbal communication is mostly summed up as body language (62%), voice tone (28%), and words (10%). In an interview, more can be said through appearance than one spoken word. Psychology studies have validated that colors have their own way of conveying images.

Many job seekers have gone through some type of "interview basics" course that tells you blue or black is the way to go. However, with an increasing amount of companies going with business casual, job seekers have become lax in their interview attire. An important thing to remember when interviewing (this includes promotions and performance reviews) is to interview for power, not position. In other words, interview for the job you want, not the position you may get. While "business casual" is becoming the norm, I would strongly advise waiting until the offer is extended and several weeks in the position, before you go with the flow - everyone is checking out the new kid. Even when you are advised this is an informal interview, for the first impression dress the part!

Psychologically speaking, let's take a look at what your colors may be saying:

BLUE - conveys peaceful, tranquil, cool, formal and sad (said to be a favorite color of most people).

BLACK - conveys authority, strength, mysterious, tragic, dignified, silent, sophisticated, evil, gloomy (be careful not to look morbid when wearing considering a black suit).

RED - conveys power, speed, hot, dangerous, passionate, angry, aggressive, or can suggest debt (how many times have you heard an accountant state, "you're in the red" and it was a positive thing?").

PURPLE - conveys royalty, dignified, powerful, dominating, dramatic, wise and passionate (it separates you from other candidates, yet it is a dark color).

YELLOW - conveys confidence, optimism, sunny, cheerful, warm, cowardly, and deceitful (stay away from it even as a tie or blouse for the interview).

GREEN - conveys friendliness, calm, cool, restful, envious, and immature (not a great first impression -- too laid back or envious).

WHITE - conveys innocence, youthful, pure, peaceful, and sterile (this in not the image you want to convey for a management position).

GRAY - conveys modest, sad, old (again, not the best choice for psychology sake).

BROWN - while in my study, I found no pro's or con's for the color brown, my personal opinion is that is conveys sturdiness, unmovable, or blends well (by all means - have at it).

Since it is a proven fact that psychology plays an important part in how others perceive us, follow the old cliché' "it's better to be seen than viewed". Take the determined effort to be seen as a professional in your industry instead of being viewed as a person who needs a professional. If you are second-guessing whether or not your wardrobe is acceptable. Decide on something else. The color of your outfit is critical, but also consider the color of your hair, nail polish, makeup and the ink pen with which you complete your application. Yes it all matters!

Okay so you have done everything right UNTIL NOW. It's time for the interview and you blow everything.

How?

NEVER

- Give too strong or too weak of a hand shake. - ouch is not equal to firm!

- Talk negatively about a previous employer.

- Arrive without pen, credentials and references.

- Offend the decision maker (or their assistant).

- Allow your temper show in the parking lot.

- Fail to hold the elevator door.

- Order alcoholic drinks during an interview (it's a test).

- Take control of the interview.

- Never be rude to the receptionist who has been with the company 10 years and can influence the decision makers.

ALWAYS

- Research the company before your arrival.

- Bring reading material of interest (and/or information you are well versed in).

- Dress for the part you want (not the part you are interviewing for).

After all, you are here to convince the employer this position was created for you - the best "me" on the planet.

Section 8
I'm the best "me" on the planet
Confidence in the Key!

Best - excelling all others

Have you ever felt the need to say something yet reserved your comment so you would not be perceived as cocky, arrogant or haughty? That is a wise choice in most situations. However, the when it is time to ask for the position, promotion or pay, you have to convey that this position was created for you - simply because YOU ARE the best on the planet.

Having confidence in who you are is critical to obtaining the future you want. Lack of self-confidence can walk you out the door as quickly as you came in. As we discussed previously, fill in the blank answers do not work. When it comes to you - you have to know who you are, know what you know and know how to stand on it.

By understanding what the interviewer is looking for within you, you have the upper hand. You have read enough books, which suggest the "correct answers" to interview questions, so we will spend this time digging "deeper than the surface". Deeper than the surface goes beyond background, dress, interview questions, education, work experience, extracurricular background and career objectives. It involves **other levels of competencies** such as:

Communication Skills
(messages, presentation, organization, interest and sincerity)

Work Ethics/Standards
(Standards of Excellence,
Responsibility and Accountability
and leaders who can encourage others)

Situational and Motivational Fit
(Job Fit (supporting visions or goals), Organizational Fit
(promotablity) and Family Fit (personal fulfillment)

Relationship Building
(Seeking profitable opportunities, developing ideas,
accomplishing goals)

Decision Making
(Identifying problems and providing solutions, detail to
information, interpreting information, appropriate follow-up
action, involvement of others)

Managing Work
(Prioritizing, scheduling, utilizes resources, staying focused)

Being "the best me on the planet" involves the ability to know who you are, what you are working with and why you must be able to convey these competencies. It sets the stage for an employer to compete for you. Possessing these competencies provide a barometer by which to measure success and are proven examples of an individual who is 'the best me on the planet". Remember what you say in the interview is only 10% of the process.

Most human resource professionals have received formal training relevant to interviewing. There are several interviewing styles developed for specific results. To determine that you have these competencies most employers utilize one or both of the following interview techniques.

- Evaluation Interviewing

Usually the human resources department, who is comparing your skills, education and organizational to the requisition and corporate culture.

- Technical Interviewing

Usually a hiring manager or co-worker skilled in the trade you are being considered will conduct the interview, i.e. an Engineering Manager interviews an Engineer.

By asking three types of questions these techniques are practiced.

- Behavioral - describing experiences or situations, which provide a picture of the reality behind the motivation.

  Example: Tell me how you won the contract?

- Theoretical - producing theories, opinions or accounts of general actions.

  Example: How would you handle conflict?

- Leading - resulting in answers that the candidate thinks you want to hear and usually prompts the correct response.

  Example: You must be proud of the fact that you have completed your degree.

Be careful of interviewers who conduct interviews without written questions. This may be a sign of an interviewer who is not effectively managing the interview process or someone without formal training in this area. This is a waste of both the candidate and the employer's time.

Just as the job seeker needs to coordinate job search efforts, interviewers should coordinate their interviewing efforts. Lack of interview coordination may indicate other areas in which the organization may also be lacking. While this not always the case, it may be a red flag and something to consider. You must also be confident in who you are so that you can interview the company. The interview serves as a time for the interviewer to interview and for you to interview the company.

In order to prepare for the competition you must do prior research by finding the company's' website, trade magazines, newspaper articles, and financial websites.
This will give you an upper hand and enough information to talk intelligently about the organization's current status and why you are an invaluable asset. Other sources to consider are: computer resources, directories, magazines, periodicals, books, and the Internet. After all, "this company is competing for you".

Part 3
PERFECT

Section 9
I am not competing for this company

Section 10
I Know What I'm Worth

Section 11
I Am Progressing

Section 12
My Skills Are Transferrable

Why Should I Hire You?

Section 9

"I'm not competing for this company, this company is competing for me"

THE JOB SEEKERS CHOICE

Company A

Company B

Company C

Compete - to strive consciously for an objective (position, profit or prize).

Now that you have told the employer you are the best you on the planet, you still have to convince them that you are the best person for the position.

If you are truly the best, up to this point, you have done everything right to gain the employers interest, don't wreck the train now. Keep going full speed until you obtain the offer you have prepared for. Many job seekers make the mistake of trying to negotiate for the position before an offer is extended. You are not a viable candidate for the position until you receive an offer of employment. Now is the time to know what you are worth without showing desperation, reservation or humiliation.

Compensation Overview

This is not for the employer, but for the job seeker. It is about understanding your worth.

Many job seekers tend to focus mainly on the net (take-home) of their paycheck. Fully understanding your worth, helps you to understand what you are "really" being paid. As a job seeker, it is important to understand your *compensation package* and not just what you take home. Regardless to the economy, know what you are worth. Without this knowledge you are cheating yourself and not reaching your full potential.

When an employer asks, "what type of salary are you looking for?" You should be able to tell them exactly <u>what</u> you are seeking and <u>why</u> you expect to be paid what you are asking for. The human resource professional knows the average salary, as well as the allowed amount the company will pay for a position. Job seekers who ask for less than what their worth - could be sending the wrong signal to the decision maker.

- You do not "really" have the experience

- You are not sure about your ability to perform

- You are not educated in your field

Job Seekers who ask for too much are also sending the wrong signals and ultimately will cost themselves great opportunities with great companies.

To be on the safe side, know the low, medium and high of the position salary and be prepared to offer a range. It is acceptable to inquire about a companies' merit system (when to expect an appraisal and possible raise) during the interview process, but do not bring up your proposed salary expectation until the employer indicates that the interview is now in "offer extended and/or negotiation stage". Knowing how the merit system works helps you to set your ducks in order when it is time to discuss salary. If you know in advance whether it will be 90 days, 6 months or 1 year before a review and possible increase, this will help you to better negotiate a starting salary that you will be comfortable with until such time.

Your salary range, of course will vary due to your individual skills set, education, experience and core competencies. Also, NEVER present yourself as an hourly employee. Always present yourself as a salaried employee. A simple way to figure this out is to take your expected hourly rate x 40 x 52. This will give you a starting range to work with. Your actual annual pay will vary based on the companies pay schedule, bonuses, merit system, and when you come onboard as an employee. The important factor is to be able to give an accurate number on the onset as opposed to when you are frustrated because you later find out find out your co-worker makes more than you.

Be mindful when choosing your information sources to gather salary information, and use at least three (3) reliable sources to gain your salary range based on your skill set, education, cost of living, etc. not solely what the position is said to pay. Understanding how to make the right additions and adjustments based on your individual skill set is key. There are many popular Internet salary sites that allow options to add a job description into their database if it does not exist.

The worse mistake a job seeker can make is to show desperation, reservation and humiliation by not understanding their worth. The consequence is life altering, because your career - by way of extension, is your life!

Employers ask employees not to discuss salaries, but we all know, it eventually comes up or somehow the information is leaked. The result creates dissension within the department, especially when there is not equal work without equal pay, or if the lesser-paid person has more skills or education. This is not always the result of a company being unfair. It is possible the higher paid co-worker knew their worth, asked for it, and got it!

When you know what you're worth, you can confidently request it and/or negotiate for it. Make sure that you do your homework. It is not always what you ask for, but how you ask for it.

When the employer asks,
"what type of salary are you looking for".

Be prepared to tell them
*"'based on my credentials, my education
and experience my expertise is valued between
this range per year".*

Successful career job seeking will also require you to be prepared to walk away when an employer doesn't value your worth. Hold on to your acceptance speech and ensure you are getting what you are worth. Jumping at the first offer extended - can also be a mistake. Always advise the employer you need to consider the offer, and do just that. You may need to evaluate your current finances, talk it over with a significant other, assess your entire employment offer, consider when you will receive your first paycheck, etc.

Always consider the offer, not just the salary. It may take you 1 hour or 1 day, but always consider the offer. Even if the employer needs someone to start tomorrow, use the ride home to consider the offer and tell the employer, you will contact him or her in 1 hour with your decision. Usually, the offer is always extended below what a company is willing to pay - with the expectation that the candidate may ask for more. If an employer doesn't value your worth now, they will not value it later (easy come-easy go).

To help with the negotiation phase, here is a chart that explains the low, medium and high salary of a paralegal.

SAMPLE POSITION
Paralegal

Provides support to attorneys. Under the direction of an attorney, resolves routine legal issues. May require an associate's degree or its equivalent and 2 years experience in the field or related area. Has knowledge of commonly used concepts, practices, and procedures within a particular field. Relies on instructions and pre-established guidelines to perform functions on the job. Works under immediate supervision usually reports to an attorney.

Based on these findings, a fare range to request would be between $33,000 and $45,000 annually.

Low - $20,040	Medium - $26,750	High - $38,240
Low - $27,112	Medium - $33,557	High - $40,579
Low - $28,700	Medium - $35,360	High - $45,010
Low - $38,085	Medium - $43,712	High - $48,875
Low - $28,574	Medium - $40,435	High - $50,479
Randomly choosing the high salary of $45,010		
Bonus 3.44% = ($1,315.46) + Benefits = ($6,976.55)		
= TOTAL COMPENSATION OF $53,534.89		

Incumbents within employment area: 731
Counties in Georgia (Barrow, Bartow, Carroll, Cherokee, Clayton, Cobb, Coweta, DeKalb, Douglas, Fayette, Forsyth, Fulton, Gwinnett, Henry, Newton, Paulding, Pickens, Rockdale, Spalding, Walton)

Additional Finding for Paralegal Salaries

Federal Government - $48,560
Legal Services - $34,230
Local Government - $34,120
State Government - $32,680

To determine the National Average Salary x (City Index as a Percentage) = Regional Average Salary. (Atlanta index number is 106.1). To calculate an estimated salary, use the index figure as percentage by moving the decimal point two places to the left. (106.1 - 1.061)

Section 10
"I know what I'm worth"

Worth - to the fullest extent of one's value or ability.

There is a difference between knowing what you want to be paid and knowing what you are worth. There are four (4) basic criteria to determine your worth.

EDUCATION - a 4-year degree is always an added bonus, but a 4-year degree is not always a requirement - depending on the employer and on the job experience. Work experience + appropriate and current certifications are sometimes equivalent to a degree, considering how educated are you in the field? In a world of consulting, employees need more than book smarts to be a viable and billable asset.

EXPERIENCE - relevant to the position you are seeking. If you are changing careers or new in a field, list transferable skills. Try not to present yourself as though all of your work experience is in the related field to obtain the current position. It will catch up to you when you are expected to know these things for efficiency.

ATTITUDE - when skill is not there, but the right attitude is - most employers will give you a chance because they see potential in you and they will be willing to train, mentor and/or coach you.

PRESENTATION - This goes back to the first impression. (your résumé, phone voice, answering machines, etc.) Be as presentable on paper as you are in person and vice versa. After all, the employer is checking you out to see if you can be presented to the organization, clients, peers or vendors, etc.

Another tidbit of information is to understand how the employer views you. You will not only interview for the position you are seeking, the base salary you expect, or the training you hope to obtain, but your overall expense to the organization. Be mindful of what you are really worth to the company, both short term and long term.

EXAMPLE
$45,010
base salary

$1548.34
(3.44%)
perks or bonus

$6976.55
(15.5%)
basic benefits

TOTAL
COMPENSATION
$53,534.89

Remember, this book was designed to help you understand and adopt the mindset of the decision maker. The employer may very well feel you are worth the $45k you are requesting, but not the $53k you are costing the company.

Are you wondering what is the big difference between $45k and $53K to a successful company? About $225k (almost a quarter of a million dollars) annually for a company employing 25 people. For each employee that is a $9k additional expense outside of the base salary. The additional $225k is for extras such as basic benefits, perks. It has no bearing on what the company still must pay for lease space, insurances, operating expenses, supplies, unemployment, etc.

If this is the expense for an organization only employing 25 people, imagine the expense for a large corporation. There is a huge difference between what you are being paid and your total compensation. Make sure you are presenting yourself as the $53k employee and not the $43k.

When you are aware of your worth. You can effectively negotiate your employment offer, even when being considered for a promotion. It is difficult to negotiate or convince the value of something unless you are educated on the product (in this case, you are the product). If you are a bargain shopper, your employer may also be.

Asking about salary information - desperation

Always let the employer bring up salary information - never ask how much the position pays. Asking about salary information shows the employer a sign of desperation. It takes away from your ability to compete and prevents you from being in a position to negotiate. It also tells the employer that your priority is "what's in it for me?" and not "what can I do for you". This can back fire - as the your needs appear to be more important than the needs of the organization.

Indicating another company is interested - reservation

Never make the employer feel pressured to make an offer to you. Telling the employer you have another offer on the table before the offer is extended shows that you may have reservations about coming on board with the employer. It may also cause the human resource professionals to second-guess themselves - after all "they are selling their product and you have chosen to shop around".

Failing to have creditable references - humiliation

Having less than creditable references will bring your entire interviewing experience to a halt. If what you say does not check out - everything you have said will be questioned. Before you go on the interview, contact your references and be sure they have a current copy of your résumé. Also be prepared to show prior paycheck stubs on the spot.

Demonstrating to the company feel like they are competing for you is to your advantage. To leverage this advantage you must know your stuff and the employer must be convinced of that. Confidence plays a major role in the final outcome. The only way to gain confidence is through proper career preparation and planning.

Confidence - a feeling or conscientiousness of one's power or reliance on one's circumstances; characterized by assurance.

By no means, is this to be construed as "Hey Mr. or Ms. Employer, you owe me because I am me", but rather "I am confident that my skill set and your organizational goal are a perfect match" - let's make it happen for mutual benefit.

Here are a few examples of how to toot your own horn during an interview and ensure your horn makes a distinct sound.

Tell me about yourself?

I am a certified job seeker with over 15 years of experience in the areas of planning, projecting, and established career goals.

Why Should I Hire You?™

I will provide your organization with the necessary skills, education and training to be successful in a position of this capacity.

Why do you want to work for this company?

I have researched your company and **I am** impressed by its stability, growth and advancement opportunities offered over the past two centuries. (Be sure to have done your homework and be ready to give actual examples of accomplishments made by the prospective employer).

Why should I choose you over the other candidates?

I am confident, based on the position discussed, my skill set and your organizational need are a perfect match.
Notice all responses began with "I" after all this interview was about "me", right? Confidence in who you are is the difference between being a public success and a private failure. On your next interview, exude confidence.

Part of your preparation is to affirm yourself by understanding "I'm not competing for this company, this company is competing for me". After all, I'm the best me on the planet. No one can beat me at being me! It cost a company thousands of dollars to hire and fire individuals. The best thing a company can do to save the bottom line is hire an individual who can grow with the company. This is the essence of being promotable and showing career progression. To an employer the ability to progress and be seen in more than one role from the onset is important.

Section 11
I am Progressing

Progress - **to develop to higher, better or more advance stage.**

If you examine Webster's definition of the word career, it does not identify success as being with the same company for any length of time, but the ability to obtain progressive achievement. Unfortunately, it is very rare to run into someone who has been the same company more than 10 years period. Somewhat due to economic changes and to a certain extent due to job seekers - job hopping. While I certainly do not advocate job hopping, it is impossible to achieve "progression" without tenacity. The point is - the mindset of how a career is viewed must change just as the times have.

When you are not promotable in company, you hear some of the statements and what here is what it really means for the job seeker.

- **Overqualified**

Can mean: we don't see you staying with our company for more than six month to one year because we will not a position in which to promote you.

- **Found someone who closely matches the position**

Can mean: (this can go either way). You may not fit into the company culture or they may not see potential in you to excel with the company.

- **Your salary range is not in our budget**

Can mean: we do think you are worth the money you are asking for or you want too much money. In some cases, they simply can not go over a certain pay rate.

To avoid hearing these responses you must demonstrate to employers that your skills are transferable.

Section 12
My Skills are Transferable

Transfer - to move, relocate, shift or reassign.

Today, many people have skills that they are not utilizing simply because they don't understand what transferable skills are. In a world where people tend to define who they are by titles and status, it is hard to see what people are really made of. It's amazing how little they know when they find themselves having to market themselves for a new career path, promotion or pay increase.

To make things a bit clearer, I am going to be totally transparent with you as we walk through my personal career path, which brings us to my current passion (preparing job seekers).

My career began as an operations assistant for a Los Angeles based engineering and construction management firm. It was a two-person office, which operated much like a staffing agency, due to the fact that our employees where usually out on project sites.

Our office was split into four divisions Accounting, Marketing, Human Resources and Operations. As an Operations Assistant, I was required to learn the daily tasks performed by the Operations Manager to ensure adequate coverage in her absence. In this environment, I learned some of the following skills.

Accounting:
Accounts payable, accounts receivable, payroll, bank reconciliation, invoice tracking, profit mark-ups, double accounting systems and monthly reporting.

Marketing:
Corporate presentations, public relations (serving as the liaison for 3 branch offices as well as the point of contact for off-site employees) creating proposals and maintaining necessary certifications.

Human Resources:
Sourcing, staffing, interviewing, recruiting, profiling employees, employee relations, performance management and compensation planning.

Operations:
Managing the day-to-day office issues, copier services, ordering supplies, processing mail, facilities and security, vendor inquiries, etc.

Administration:
Along with my corporate responsibilities, the owner of the company received an appointed position from President Bill Clinton within the Federal Home Loan Bank and all the related correspondence, arranging his travel and the likes, fell on my desk.

While this was certainly an overwhelming position, especially for the pay - in retrospect, I am grateful that I was afforded the opportunity to be cross-trained in the five areas discussed early in my career. It provided me with a foundation to make clear decisions about the career choices I would have to make. I knew that accounting was not it. Of the five areas, I was felt the most fulfilling are of responsibility when dealing with people and choose to pursue a career in human resources.

My next position was an administrator for the largest credit card manufacturer in the world. In a manufacturing company with 400+ employees, and due to the structure of the organization, I was the closest thing to a traditional administrative assistant, providing support to the Company president, VP of Human Resources and Administration, marketing managers and the client services department. Department. While I was challenged with constant deadlines, I enjoyed this position because it was never dull, but it certainly was not a 9-5. For obvious security reasons, company operations were distributed between three locations (Building 1 - the cards were ordered, Building 2 - the cards were embossed and Building 3 - the cards were shipped). The structure of the company greatly challenged my ability to prioritize was the largest area of responsibility. Everyone needed what they needed now! Let's take a look at some of my duties and task:

Client Services - First point of contact for all customer issues, administering correspondence, research and inputting, sending out proofs, etc.

Human Resources - Applicant testing and sourcing, interviewing, payroll, benefit administration, time and attendance, employee relations meetings, etc.

Administration - Reports and correspondence for the Company President, VP of Administration, and marketing Managers, handle all telecommunication issues, arrange travel, employee relations, and handle all logistics for trade shows.

The need to set priorities developed a keen sense to evaluate effectiveness without waste. For several months, I kept track of my daily tasks and unreasonable requests. During my performance review, I was able to clearly show my employer that my load was unbalanced, I was over-worked, under-paid and convince my employer that I needed help. Because I was able to handle my tasks successfully, my employer did not realize all the work was had been piled on me. Impressed that I was able to carry such a load, yet seeing that I was drowning in work, my review warranted the hiring of an Executive Assistant to take on some of my responsibilities and my promotion as Assistant to the Vice President of Administration and Human Resources. In this position, I honed in on my human resource disciplines and gained progressive experience.

From this point on, I was employed strictly in the human resource environment, where I gained a full understanding of the many human resource disciplines including human resource planning, job analysis and design, staffing and recruitment, including college recruiting, selection, performance evaluation and management, compensation, employee benefits, VISA Issues, training and development, career planning and development, employee discipline, safety and health, staffing and college recruiting. Several years later, I did end up resigning from this employer, and to date (six years later), I still maintain a positive relationship with several people within the organization, including my former boss.

My only reason for leaving this employer was to accept a new position an Operations Manager (which included Administration and Human Resources) and a huge salary by a company that was "competing for me". I interviewed and corresponded with this agency for organization for several months. Before accepting this position, I spent many evening talking with the employer, attending some of their workshops, meeting their clients, etc. After the offer was extended, I took few weeks vacation from my current employer to spend time with my new potential employer. This was the best career plan I could have devised. I was able to clearly see the daily operations and inform my employer before hand what I would need to reach my career goals. Because I was in a position where the company was competing for me, I was able to convince the   employer that I was an asset not just a liability (as human resources is rarely viewed as profit center).

I did not share this information to boast on my career experience, but to make a point. I worked very hard in my career for other people and it has prepared me for the tasks that come with being a business owner. I fully understand the levels of sacrifice required to be successful. The type of positions I held required working extended hours, weekends, and odd hours that no one else wanted to work, without the option of discussion - it just has to be done! I have provided the following examples of how my previous experience built the transferable skills necessary for my current functions.

Here are a few transferable skills:

Tasks	Transferable Skill:	Lesson Learned:
Accounting	Maintaining appropriate bookkeeping, taxes and payroll issues.	Accuracy is necessary to keep my business afloat, and maintain relationships with banks, employees and customers.
Marketing	Creating a professional imagine and being able to sell my company and its services to my prime market.	The perception that people have based on my presentation is a deciding factor
Human Resource Management	I understand all aspects and have the inside knowledge that job seekers need to gain the upper hand in their career endeavors.	Gained the insight to align human assets with organizational goals.
Operations	I have worked for Fortune 500 companies and learned many do's and don't necessary to stay in business as well as maintain repeat business from customers/clients.	Systems must be in place and plans must be followed to become a leader in the industry.
Clients Services	Superb customer service!	Without customers I have no business.
Administration	Ability to make the best business purchases and decisions based on previous usage of services and fees.	How to be effective without waste.

Performance Evaluations	Help job seekers set clear career goals, It's a do or die!	The ability to evaluate work habits and determine strengths, weaknesses and area devise plans to meet career goals.

The exceptional thing about my career path is that my education, training and experience also opens the door for other career opportunities and related occupations such as; counselor, education administrator, public relations specialists, psychologist or a social worker.

These are the kind of things you find out during career planning sessions. See, I told you...career continuation is a lifestyle for a lifetime. As a job seeker your objective in your current position is to set a career plan that enables you to find your transferable skills and determine how they will enhance your career.

Part 4
Settle

Section 13
Career Planning

Section 14
Recycled Resources

Section 15
Excellent References Upon Request

Section 16
I've Learned From My Mistakes

Section 13
Career Planning

Career - A field for or pursuit of consecutive progressive achievement.

Planning - the act or process of making or carrying our plans.

The ability to successfully compete with other job seekers increases when you have a plan for success. When planning your career you will find the nature of work, tasks, knowledge, skills, abilities, work activities, work context, job zones, interest, work values, work needs, working conditions, occupational specialty, training and certifications needed, advancement opportunities, job outlook, earning potential, and most importantly related occupations importantly career related fields.

EXAMPLE

Human resource manager credentials are transferable skills for a counselor, education administrator, public relations specialist, social worker and psychologist. Of course these skills occupations require some additional education, but they open the door.

Career Development and Progression Plan

Once you have determined what career you wish to pursue, it is time to become accountable and execute a plan of action. This is a more in-depth goal setting process as it will become your life or determine how you live it.

EXAMPLE

A human resource manager should posses a bachelor's degree in human resources, business administration or a related field and a human resource certification is a plus. They must also have 3-5 years of human resource generalist experience and have a sound understanding of employment laws, general business practices, training, compensation and recruiting.

If these things are not part of your current track record, the chances of you being selected for a human resource manager position are slim. This may be an opportunity to step into a position which allows you to build on human resource functions (training, recruiting, payroll), but understanding these are function of human resources and not full cycle human resource management. But knowing what you need to do to obtain this position is have the battle. If you know that you want to become a human resource manager, you are now aware of what steps you need to take to achieve that goal.

SAMPLE CAREER PROGRESSION PLAN
(for a current HR Administrator or Generalist seeking to be a HR Manager)

ACTION ITEM	TIMELINE
Read Industry related material and subscribe to business publications	On-going
Continue education and complete required courses	On-going
Join HR Organization for Training and Mentorship	Now
Obtain Generalist Certification	August 2000
Complete degree in Business Administration	June 2003
Obtain HR Manager Certification (CHRM or PHR)	December 2003
State your career aspirations and request more HR Manager duties during your performance review	January 2004
Apply for HR Manager position	June 2005

Find someone who will help you stay on track, hold you accountable to your timelines and encourage your career aspirations. This can be a mentor, spouse, parent, colleague, or a career planning and development agency, such as P.H.D. Career Strategies.

If your current employer does not have the opportunity you are seeking and once you complete your employability toolbox, you are now ready to become marketable for another employer!

Section 14
I recycle my resources"

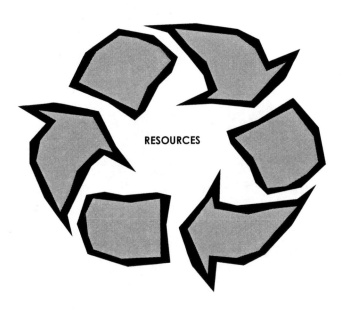

RESOURCES

Recycle - to adapt to a new use
Resource - a source of supply or support

Hopefully by now you are adopting the mindset of the job seeker and you are ready to executive your plan of action.

In preparing for job seeking yourself you will need to know the answers to the following questions:

- Where are the jobs?
- Who do I talk to?
- Does this align with my career plan?

Where are the jobs? - Everywhere!
Job seekers have the responsibility of getting noticed. A position is not going to drop out of the sky. Surfing the net and reading the want ads is good - but not your best. Research conducted by Spherion showed the following areas to be to be key referral sources for employment.

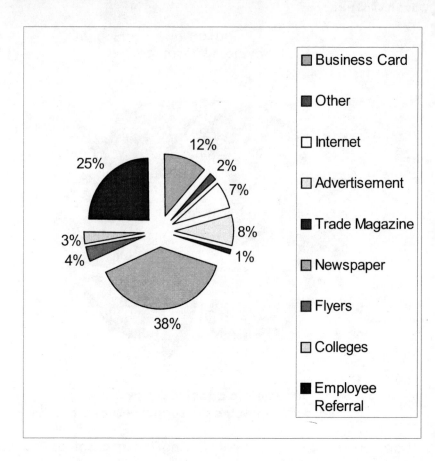

While, the newspaper is the leading referral source for job seeker, the referral alone will not guarantee a position. Job seekers cannot stop at the most common referrals. Relying on these common referrals is job seeking by what some call the iceberg analogy.

What is the iceberg analogy? Imagine a frozen body of water. The top layer is frozen solid (10%), but the water underneath is not (90%). What does this mean to the job seeker? If you only seeking solid layers, you are spending 90% of your time seeking only 10% of available positions. Doing so limits your employment options.

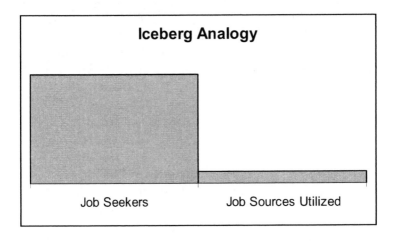

Economic recovery will paychecks in the hands of millions, many who are unemployed or on welfare. Career education and unemployment will not only allow new avenues for employment, it will also assist individuals in life skill areas that are exceeding difficult to master.

Take a position in the help wanted section of your local paper, for example. Ads are normally placed on Sunday and Wednesday, but have you considered how many candidates can preview the ad and apply for it? The number is not measurable. An individual in Alaska can apply for the position just as easy as a local candidate with the use of technology. We have already determined that studies prove only 6-7% of management positions are obtained through Internet job boards so where are the other jobs?

Some are still in your local papers, just not where you are accustomed to looking. Here are 20 proven alternative places job seekers can find employment, that are not in the "help wanted" section.

1. Articles - The Atlanta Business Chronicle ran an article titled "Managing Human Resources" (date here). In the article, the human resource manager of a major bank indicated there were currently over 1,000 job openings.

2. New Business - Many papers list new business license and/or articles of incorporations being issued. The information also provides key contact information such as the company name, locations and the owners name and phone number. New business = employees.

3. Developments - Contact developers and see where they are in the development stages of their project. Even if you didn't plan to clean or decorate new homes for a living, a developer may agree to pay you $300 per home to clean or decorate. This new development has 100 homes - you do the math. $30,000 per development project!!!

4. Follow the money - Publications such as Venture Reporter list when companies receive funding. More money equals more work and a need for more staff.

5. Put your job on reserve (layaway)- This is a creative way of networking. Start going to business meetings, luncheons and association meetings and make people begin to "wonder" who you are. You must be somebody; after all...you're at EVERY meeting. Trust me, people will approach you and you better be ready to sell your skills.

6. Leasing Agents - Make an appointment with commercial leasing agents and tell them "I am considering doing business here". Find out what other businesses are in the building and who the decision makers are.

7. Become a door-to-door salesman - Get up, get dressed and get out of the house! Drive around and go door-to-door requesting to speak with the Human Resource Manager (do your homework so you can ask for him or her by name). Be sure to leave your "resu-card™". Ask for the business card of the human resource manager and then follow up with your résumé.

8. Make the delivery - Well, it can be anyone who delivers FedEx, UPS, U.S. postal carrier, or the water man, usually they work the same route and develop relationships with people on their route. Small talk sometimes leads to invaluable information. Pay them to "deliver the goods for you".

9. Industry promotions - Let's say you are a repair technician, contact other repair technicians and tell them you are job seeking and you want to know who there top clients are.

10. Set up a contest - This may appeal more to the entrepreneur, but it works for job leads as well. Create a promotion that showcases your skill set. You will receive many business cards and contacts, which have now become prospective employers. Be sure that you promote something that you can follow through with.

11. Find a business mentor - If there is an industry you desire to pursue period. Find someone who is established in the industry and offer to be their assistant (yes for free). They will have first hand knowledge of your work and be able to either hire you or recommend you.

12. Volunteer/Intern - Get involved with organizations that may be short staffed and offer your assistance. When the opportunity permits the organization to be in a position to hire, it will be much easier to hire someone who is already in place and understands the job, culture and the responsibility.

13. Take the job! - If you recall earlier in the book, we defined job as "occasional pieces of work". Sometimes you may need to take a "job" to make ends meet. However, see this as an opportunity to seek out other employment opportunities within the organization. Let the employer know that you would like to be considered for a position with the company that offers growth. This is not a conversation to have on day one, but filter the work load and find the right time to have the conversation. For those of you who are working through temporary agencies, hold on, many opportunities can arise when you do an exceptional job as a temporary talent.

14. Go back to school - Additional education can provide career advancement and opportunity. It also shows the employer that you are willing to continue learning. A sign that every employer looks for in a leader.

15. Internet posting - Choose industry specific sites to post your résumé accordingly. This allows your résumé to be seen by employers who you were not aware had an opening. These employers are actively seeking employer and just may find your résumé on the Internet. This is a creative way to let your résumé work for you while you work for others.

16. Talk to the boss - During your performance evaluation share your career aspirations with your boos. Ask your boss to consider you for upcoming positions and if they will find someone within the organization to mentor you. This mentor may also be someone outside of the organization that your boss may be able to connect you to. Your performance evaluation is a time to lay things on the table. Assess where you are in your career, with your current employer and set career goals to strive for. If your current evaluations do not offer goals to strive for, you may want to consider other options. If an employer does not set goals for your future performance, it may be difficult to prove later that you have made or can make a significant contribution.

17. Write your own ticket - Once you have been mentored and have identified the need of the organization, demonstrate how your skill set is a perfect match by creating your own position based on the need identified.

18. Email blast - Use the contacts in your email address book to send out your credentials. Ask your contacts to share with their contacts - continue to do this often until you receive a response. Add some humor; be sure to inform them, if they don't send your résumé to at least 10 people within 24 hours, they will have bad luck ☺. It works on forwards and jokes, why not try it with a résumé.

19. **Build a website** - Build an HTML flyer about your credentials and include a link to your personal website. Be sure the website holds only pertinent career information on your skill set and ability. The same rules apply here as they would for résumés. Refrain from using any personal information that can be used to discriminate against you such as: pictures, marital status, hobbies, children, gender, etc.

20. **Resu-card™ Networking** - your resu-card can be exchanged with anyone, anywhere and anytime. Successfully utilizing professional prepared resu-cards to showcase your skill set makes all the difference, makes all the difference. Self made, flimsy, perforated cards with poor paper quality and ink jet printing will certainly serve as a career derailment. This is an inexpensive, highly effective method of branding yourself in a positive way.

Who do I talk to? - Everyone!
Break out of the social norm. Post 9-11, it is not uncommon "I'm unemployed". Tell everyone who will listen. WHY? Everyone knows someone who knows someone else. Studies have proven that 61% of management level employment opportunities comes from networking. Networking is a powerful tool, if used correctly, you will not be unemployed for long. There is no special recipe to networking; there is a simple process of telling everyone you come in contact with about your skill set.

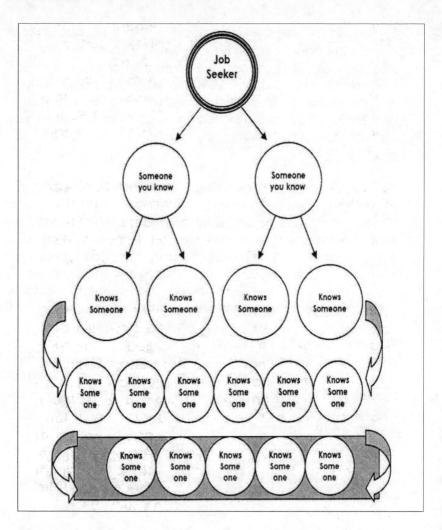

Does this fit into my career plan? - Eventually!

Sometimes it will, sometimes it won't, sometimes, it will later! It depends on the level of sacrifice you are willing to make to reach your ultimate career goal. Let me pause here and share a new perspective on a career.

After 10 years of seeing the need first hand, my passion to educate job seekers on the recruiting process grew. I knew that I wanted to own my own business. Considering that I had just broken free from repaying school loans, the last thing I wanted to do was obtain a bank loan. So I found alternative ways to create cash flow to obtain my career aspirations. It was not easy, nor did it happen overnight.

The first thing to change was my mindset. I had to worry less about what was wrong or right with my current employment situation and focus more on what was important to me! (not my mother, father, or friends, etc.) I WANTED MY OWN BUSINESS! So I made the appropriate investments to make it happen.

The next set of things to changed was my priorities - everything I did, or thought of doing, I questioned. Is this going to get me closer to my goal, or delay my goal? My decision making process became easy. My social habits changed, my social circle changed and my social views changed. I began to do extensive market research. I was encouraged when I found that I could offer the same or better services than the industry leaders. I wrote a business plan, gave up my "corporate comforts", and put my plans into action.

After all, I was looking to fulfill my career goal not find a job. People will tell you there is no such thing as a career these days, but I tend to disagree. Webster defines career as "progressive advancement in a field" as long as you are advancing in your field or industry you are certainly on the right career track. So what's in a C-A-R-E-E-R?

C - Choices
I decided I no longer wanted to be an employee, but an employer. I learned the value of operating from the bottom up and saw that I had an opportunity to impact lives. Every choice I made had a direct reflection on my ability to turn my dreams into details.

A - Assessment
I had to look at completing my employability toolbox and evaluate my career progression. I was at a corporate level that would require more traveling than I was willing to do or could afford to do and still reach my goals. Being on the road and

working 12-hour days would make it impossible for me to reach my personal career aspirations - like write this book.

So I began to assessment my skills, obtain additional credentials and market myself as a consultant. I was in a position where my decisions did not affect anyone but me so this was the perfect time to go after my dream. My assessment was both professional and personal.

R - Research
Market Research was invaluable. Even more so, when I did it myself. It provided the insight find first hand the strengths and weaknesses of industry leaders. It also provided a secure foundation, which is the difference between failure and success.

E - Explore
I worked three (3) years as a consultant to experience working in various industries and company sizes. This afforded me the income to maintain my lifestyle as well as the flexibility to make my own schedule.

E - Execution
My business plan was my guide. It includes short term and long terms goals with completion dates. I established an advisory board so that I would be accountable to someone and I began to do what I love - work with job seekers.

R - Responsibility
I realized that I had the responsibility to become the creator of my work life, shaping it, instead of reacting to it. The capacity to view things in their relative importance is extremely vital for the job seeker.

To answer the questions posed at the beginning of this chapter

Where are the jobs?
Who do I talk to?
Does this align with my career plan?

It takes time, preparation, resources and references.

Section 15
"Excellent References Available Upon Request"

Excellent - To surpass an accomplishment or achievement (excel)

References - a person to whom inquires as to character or ability can be made.

Many job seekers pass every test and then fail to pass a reference check. References can work for you or against you. When a company chooses to conduct a reference check, the credibility of your reference influences the hiring decision.

Let's examine what I call "Influential References". These are references that influence the hiring decision that you never put .down on paper. Here are a few "real-world", scary stories that certainly influenced my decision during the hiring process. These are not made-up examples, but things I have actually experienced in my career.

1. The significant other

While recruiting for a company, which offered relocation to Engineers. I called a candidate located in another state with a different time zone. I could tell by his résumé that he was currently employed so I waited until about 7 p.m. to call him at home (hint - do not attempt to talk with potential employers while at your current place of employment - certainly you can not speak freely - and you are presenting a first impression). His significant other picked up the phone.

When I asked to speak to him, she responded with an offensive "who is this?" I explained my position and reason for the call. She went on to tell me that no one called at 7 p.m. to conduct a phone interview and hung up on me. I did not call back and of course, he did not get the position.

2. The teenager

We found the perfect candidate for a client who intended to interview over the next two days and make an immediate decision. I made contact with a job seeker to ensure he was available for an on-the-spot interview. I told him I needed to finalize a few things with my client's availability and would confirm the time that he should report to his interview.

I called six times and each time, the teenage daughter told me to "call him back" when I told her that I had already called several times and I needed to speak with him regarding an interview she said "okay well hang up, call back and I wont answer and you can leave him a message". The problem was, the client wanted to see him in an hour. Needless to say he did make the interview.

3. The toddler

I called and asked to speak with Mr. Doe. The toddler laughed and hung up. I called again and said "can I speak to mommy". She said "no" and hung up again. I called again and asked to speak to daddy. She said "no daddy" and hung up. Needless to say, after making 3 calls no adult intervened. . Third strike - candidate out!

4. The roommate

I called to conduct a phone screen and the roommate told me "he is not here, I just got off work and I don't feel like getting up to get a pen". Call him back tomorrow afternoon. Needless to say, I had a stack of résumés and simply choose to call the next candidate who promptly picked up the phone.

5. The background

Be mindful of the baby crying, people talking loud, the TV blasting. When you are taking an important call, it is best to remove yourself from the action. It is totally acceptable to tell the employer "one moment please, I need to take this call in another room".   Needless to say, so often job seekers fail to adhere to this and show their lack of control in the home environment, leaving the employer an opportunity to question if they can handle the office environment.

6. Past employer

There is only one option to consider; how you left the employer. When you leave correctly - you can always come back - even it's just for a reference. Be sure that you never burn bridges to an employer you may need in the future. Even if you are terminated, leave correctly - it can affect your future.

When an employee is terminated, they tend to use past co-workers and friends who are still with the company. On a professional note (for me), this would send up a red flag and I would go the extra step to look up the number and call the Human resources department directly. If the exit from your past employer was less than graceful, it is not wise to list friends and co-workers as references. This can back fire for a few reasons. Seasons and friendships change, just as employment conditions. The flip side to this is to list employers who cannot remember who you are - because you never came out of your cubicle. It is not a creditable reference when an employer cannot recall who you are. Granted, the companies' point of contact can and will change, but your records need to be consistent with their records.

7. Fabrication of information

The areas in which most résumés are fabricated in tenure and titles. This information is verified and makes everything on your résumé seem questionable when simple things don't match. For instance, your records show 1 year, the employers record shows 1 month.

8. Answering Machine

Be professional period! You choice of music, your sense of humor, and your enunciation may all be offensive. Needless to say how you represent your home (including the cell phone) is an indication of how you may represent the organization.

Influence goes a long way. Your goal is to project yourself as the consummate professional and be considered the best person to bring into an organization. While you may not consider these instances to serve as references, a human resource professional may. These are just a few items to consider about references, telling you other stories, would be a separate book!

These are just a few examples to be cognizant of. These are not references you want an employer to obtain while considering you for hire. During your job search, you must become "a professional job seeker" 24 hours a day. Be extra careful not to offend the person calling. You never know what is or is not offensive to the person on the other end. The ability to be in control of your personal environment brings into question whether or not you can control your professional environment. This can prove to be a mistake that can not be fixed.

Section 16
I've learned from my mistakes.

Mistake - A wrong action or settlement proceeding from faulty judgment. Inadequate knowledge or ill intentions.

Regardless to your skill, knowledge or education there are typically three (3) life mistakes which can affect your ability to become or remain gainfully employed.
These are the three (3) deadly C's to the employment process.

1. Credit Report

Many employers use a credit report as a vital source when determining employability. Most job seekers will learn how credit relates to employment through trial and error. Being privileged to see the adverse affect first hand, I tend to disagree that the three deadly C's alone accurately paint a clear picture of a candidate's character or ability to perform in a position based on the following reasons:

70% of undergraduates have credit cards.

In most cases, campuses receive money for allowing credit card representatives to come out. In this vain, credit card marketing can be compared to college students what

101

tobacco marketing is to minors. They have the opportunity to experience the process without understanding the long-term consequences.

It is almost impossible to keep a satisfactory credit rating without an income to pay creditors. As a human resource professional, I was not trained to read a credit report as part of the selection process, but was forced to make a judgment call on a person's ability to perform based on a report. Unfortunately, it is a reality that many job seekers, bad credit cripples their work life. Many do not understand how to read a credit report and the job seeker is not afforded the opportunity to explain situations such as divorce, death, illness, loss of employment, just to name a few things can could be impact your credit rating.

An employer who pulls a credit report for employment purposes is required to inform an applicant of the fair credit reporting act. The verbiage will read something like this:

"this report if obtained may contain information baring your credit worthiness, good standing, credit capacity, character, criminal background, driving history, general reputation, personal characteristics or mode of living."

The purpose of the report is to determine if you are a viable candidate for:

- Employment
- Promotion
- Re-assignment
- Placement (or)
- Retention as an employee

However because a credit report is often misread this is more harmful to the job seeker than good. The best thing a job seeker can do is clear their credit history as part of preparing for a career.

If you have a past credit rating less than favorable, the first goal upon obtaining employment (even temporary work) is to begin to pay off small accounts.

An employer is required to notify you when you are denied employment as a result of your credit rating. This provides you with a small window of opportunity to give the employer a rebuttal (and proof) that you are responsible enough to pay off your debts or at least making an effort to do so.

2. Criminal History

- Workplace discrimination (adversely affects minorities).

Even without a criminal history minorities are sometimes looked over. A study by Northwest University showed that 17% of white ex-cons are called back for interviews compared to 14% of crime-free black candidates.

Workplace Discrimination	
Percentage of job applicants who get called back after the initial interview.	
Black	White
With criminal record 5%	With criminal record 14%
Without criminal record 14%	Without criminal record 34%

Source: Devah Pager, Northwest University

While this same study revealed the "Emily and Greg are 50% more employable than "Lakisha and Jamal" simply due to having less ethnic sounding names, these states translate into the need for minorities to mail 15 résumés to every 20 résumés sent my non-minorities in order to land one (1) interview.

Statistics clearly show that workplace discrimination takes places in more than one area and minorities are less likely to be chosen for some career opportunities based on a background check and simply the review of a name, which in required for the check.

Legislative talks in regards to the adverse affects on minorities in the workplace being an unfair practice have surfaced but fighting such discrimination will require additional funding for enforcement agencies so we'll have to hold on and see how things pan out.

If you are a minority job seeker with an ethnic or Arabic or other name that may be discriminated against, try using a middle name when applying for positions. Example, if the name is LaKisha Nicole, consider L. Nicole or Nicole.

Many employers are not willing to take a chance on employees with a criminal background. The irony of this is these days you can be placed in jail or have your license suspended for not having means to pay child support and/or traffic tickets. I think employers should do more research on the specifics of a person's record to fully understand the consequences. In some instances, people may simply make a bad choice once in a lifetime and society does not give the opportunity to be redeemed (thank God for Jesus!).

There is a difference between a career criminal and a person who make a poor choice. While I do believe a person should be held responsible for the choices they make. I also believe every choice has a circumstance attached to it and should be considered. Some choices are forced on others that is beyond their control. Some choices are a way of life, proven by repeat behavior.
If you are a first offender, be sure that is your last offense. Make all attempts necessary to have your record expunged once you have completed your sentence or probation. This is not a way around your past, but a way to show that you have certainly learned from your mistakes and ready to do the right thing.

3. Character References

- Whatever the past, the most influential reference is your past employer.

A good name is to be chosen than riches. It is up to you to keep in contact with the people whom you list as references. They need to know you by name. Call and advise your references that you are job seeking and send a current copy of your résumé.

I once heard a wise man say "when you leave right, you can always come back." It may not be for continued employed but a satisfactory reference helps you to remain gainfully employed. While there are some employers you may wish you had never encountered by all means, when you need to leave do so with professionalism and tact or it may come back to haunt you.

For those of you are new to the work force and do not have previous employment as references, you will want to use personal references and indicate them as such. Choose these personal reference carefully. Avoid using family friends that can not validate any work ethic.

Human resource professionals call references even those you do not list. While these are all influential references, they are not the type of influence you want a potential employer to have when deciding whether or not you are the best person to bring into an organization. While you may not consider these examples to serve as references, a human resource professional may.

When an employer makes a call to you be respectful and show that you appreciate their time. The time they have taken to review your qualifications, consider you for a position and reach out to you. Be sure that you avail yourself to meet the employer's convenience.

Part 5
Employable and Promotable

Section 17
I Understand The Recruiting Process

Section 18
My Résumé Is With The Right Source

Section 19
I Am Promotable

Section 20
I Am The Missing Piece To The Puzzle

Section 17
I understand the recruiting process

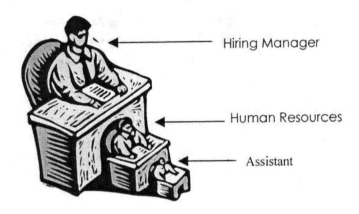

Hiring Manager

Human Resources

Assistant

Recruiting - the process of adding new individuals to a population.

Process - a series of actions or operations conducing to an end.

This section is not to be confused with the differences between HR Professionals, Recruiters, and Staffing agencies. Regardless to the separate industry segments, all three (3) must have a recruiting process.

A huge part of understanding the process for the job seeker is to be available when an employer is attempting to make contact. A study by Sperion Pacific Enterprises LLC showed the following to be the best times to reach candidates.

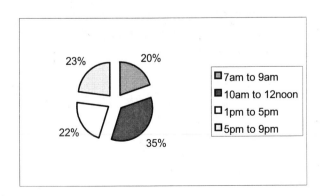

A job seeker should be aware that the best time to call an employer to inquire about an opening may not be 8:00 am. For the job seeker using a staffing agency 8:00 am maybe the best time to call in your availability.

Notice, from this study, the best time to reach a candidate begins at 10:00 am. So what does that mean for the job seeker? The person you are trying to reach is going to be sitting at their desk 35% of the time between the hours of 10am and 12 noon in job seeker mode. This also means that you are catching them at a convenient time to talk. Also note, from this study that the second best time to reach candidates is from 5pm to 9pm. Which means that businesses conduct job-seeking operations outside the "normal 9am to 5pm" and job seekers must be prepared for this.

Before we preview the entire process, I want to point out the roles played during the recruiting process.

In some cases the human resource professional is the decision maker who starts and controls the process. The hiring manager usually selects whom they want to hire within their department, relying on the input of the human resource professional. The recruiting process is a series of necessary step used to eliminate candidates who are not in the running for the open position.

The unfortunate thing is candidates themselves create a larger portion of areas to be of disqualified. Here are the top five (5) reasons, which disqualify candidates.

3% Self elimination (Unemployable)
20% lack of related job related experience
43% Requesting Flexible Schedules
15% No Legal Right to Work
16% No not posses valid Driver's License

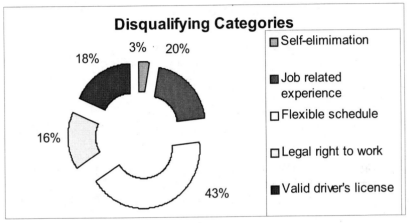

Disqualifying Categories

3%   20%
18%

16%

43%

- Self-elimimation
- Job related experience
- Flexible schedule
- Legal right to work
- Valid driver's license

(Source Spherion)

Can you imagine being picky about schedule, when you are unemployed? An alarming 43% are counting themselves out usually due to "can't work the weekends".

While these are the top five (5) reasons candidates are eliminated from the recruiting process, there are other areas of elimination to be considered. Because there are more candidates than positions.

Before any decision is made to hire, a process of candidate elimination must take place. This usually involves the hiring manager, human resources and an assistant, where applicable. Depending on the procedures in place, the assistance can be the first point of contact.

It is important that all parties who see your résumé can evaluate it for core competencies and not just use a simple criteria selection mode. It is up to the job seeker to understand the recruiting process by creating documents that showcase a winning skill set regardless to the submission mode used.

Other Elimination Factors

- Internal candidate selected for the position
- Not paying attention to details
  (no cover letter sent not including salary information)
- Poor quality of a résumé
- Being a pest during the interview process
- Unable to be contacted for a phone screen
- Offensive music on the answering machine
- Greeted rudely by others answering the telephone
- Can not articulate what is on your résumé
- Putting past employers down
- Burning bridges
- Late to an interview
- Rude to the receptionist and other current employees
- Excuses for being late - just tell the truth
- Presentation (unprofessionally dressed, wrinkled, sloppy)
- Interview Poorly
  (62% body language 28% voice tone 10% words)
- Résumé is fabricated
- References don't check out
- Desperation - asking about money turns the employer off
- Employee referrals from a terrible employee
- To relaxed or too tense in the interview
- Out of sight, out of mind (send a thank you note)
- Not a company fit (everyone is not employable)

Another way to ensure you are not eliminated from the recruiting process is to make sure your résumé is with the right source.

Section 18
My résumé is with the right source.

Source - a generative source

To help you determine the right source for your career path we will examine the various skill set, functions and differences between the human resource professional, recruiter, and the staffing agent.

While recruiting, staffing, and payroll are functions of human resources, it is not the same as full cycle human resource management. In addition to recruiting, staffing and payroll a human resource professional has more responsibility such as: compliance, job analysis, labor relations, policy/procedures, strategic planning, and health and safety to name a few. Here is a chart to show some differences that can exist.

Individual Functions of HR	Full Cycle HRM (includes functions to the left)
Recruiting/staffing Payroll Benefit administration Training/development Labor relations	Performance Management Compliance Coordination Job Analysis Organizational Development HR Planning (forecasting) Safety, health and wellness Career Planning Reports Restructuring Compensation

While every function of human resources is important and each serve a unique purpose. It is vitally important for job seekers to understand that a human resource professional may recruit, but a recruiter may not be a human resource professional, but rather one who handles a function of human resources.

Let's explore the advantages and disadvantages:

Human Resource Mangers

Plan, direct and coordinate human resource management activities of an organization to maximize the strategic use of human resources and maintain functions such as employees' compensation, recruitment, personnel policies, and regulatory compliance.

ADVANTAGES

1. Hired to bring the best people in house for productivity and profit.

2. Have formal training in recruiting, staffing, compensation and other areas of human resource management.

3. Thoroughly interviews candidates for best overall fit in the company, as this reflects their performance.

DISADVANTAGES

1. Slower to hire due to in house process.

2. Follow company culture when hiring as opposed to selecting "the most qualified" individual.

3. Human Resource departments candidate of choice is often over ruled by hiring managers choice (human resources interview for the best company fit, while hiring managers interview for best technical fit).

Recruiters (or Headhunters)

Screens, interviews, and recommends prospective employees for employment. Extends offers of employment to successful candidates. Has knowledge of commonly-used concepts, practices, and procedures within a particular field. While they are more sales driven than a staffing agency, they too have a goal in mind and a bottom line dollar figure. Most recruiters are corporate based or self-employed contractors.

Staffing Agents (or Employment Interviewers)

Interviewing job applicants in employment office and refer them to prospective employers for consideration. Search applicant files, notify selected applicants of job opening, and refer qualified applicants to prospective employers.

ADVANTAGES
both RECRUITERS AND STAFFING AGENTS

1. Flexibility to create various work schedules.

2. Exposure to careers and companies you may not consider or know of vacancies within.

3. Try to gain higher salaries to increase their commission.

4. Will submit you to multiple companies simultaneously.

DISADVANTAGES

1. Limited career planning and development options.

2. Do not build lasting relationship with talent.

3. Submit multiple candidates to compete for the same position - puts them in a position to negotiate on their behalf (not the job seeker).

4. Sales driven more so than career driven.

5. Use large career boards, hard for employer to pick you out.

According to the Occupational Information Network, www.salary.com and Randstad there are distinct differences in the skill set and function between the three:

HUMAN RESOURCE MANAGER 5 to 7 years of Generalist Experience Required Reports to an Executive Requires a Bachelor's Degree Implements Program and Policies Designs and Plans Relies on experience and judgment to accomplish goals Pay: Salary + Bonus (Also responsible for staffing, compensation, benefits, VISA/green cards, employee relations, training, health and safety programs).

Human Resource Manager:

1. Administer compensation, benefits and performance management systems, and safety and recreation programs.

2. Advise managers on organizational policy matters such as equal employment opportunity and sexual harassment and recommend needed changes.

3. Allocate human resources, ensuring appropriate matches between personnel, identify staff vacancies and recruit, interview and select applicants.

4. Perform difficult staffing duties, including dealing with understaffing, refereeing disputes, firing employees and administering disciplinary procedures.

5. Provide current and prospective employees with information about policies, job duties, working conditions, wages, and opportunities for promotion and employee benefits.

RECRUITER (or Headhunter)
0-3 years experience
Works under Supervision
May Require a Bachelor's Degree
Has knowledge of commonly used concepts
Relies on instruction and pre-established guidelines
Relies on experience and judgment
Pay: Salary or Commission

Recruiters (or Headhunters)

1. Perform searches for qualified candidates according to relevant job criteria, using computer databases, networking, Internet recruiting, resources, cold calls, media, recruiting firms, and employee referrals.

2. Consider the relative cost and benefits of potential actions to choose the best candidate for their clients.

3. Contact applicants to inform them of employment possibilities, consideration, and selection.

4. Evaluate recruitment and selection criteria to ensure conformance to professional, statistical, and testing standards, recommending revisions as necessary.

5. Inform potential applicants about facilities, operations, benefits, and job or career opportunities in organizations.

STAFFING AGENTS (or Employment Interviewers)
3 - 5 years work experience in
Reports to an Executive
Requires a Bachelor's Degree
Previous Sales Representative
or Management Experience
Relies on sales ability
Pay: Salary + Bonus

ADVANTAGES

1. Flexibility to create a schedule that works for you.

2. Various work experience and see different working environments.

3. Exposure to careers you may not consider without the opportunity to work in the industry.

DISADVANTAGES

1. No long term or career planning options for the talent.

2. Testing systems are outdated and do not give an employer an accurate picture of your skill set (i.e....you are use to working with Windows 2000 and they test you on Windows 98, you want to use a short cut to execute the command and the computer marks your answer as incorrect).

3. You are not paid your worth (the agency bills you at $15 per hour and you receive $10 per hour).

Recruiters (headhunters)

Note: headhunters are usually self-employed high end recruiters.

Staffing (or Employment Interviewers)

1.   Contact employers to solicit orders for job vacancies, determining their requirements and recording relevant data such as job descriptions.

2.   Hire workers and place them with employers needing temporary help.

3. Review employment applications and job orders to match applicants with job requirements, using manual or computerized file searches.

4.   Conduct and arrange testing of applicants and current employees.

5.   Interview job applicants to match their qualifications with employers' needs, recording and evaluating applicant experience, education, training and skill.

According to www.salary.com and Randstad here are other differences to compare:

HR Manager www.salary.com	Recruiters www.salary.com	Staffing Agents Randstad.com
7 years experience Reports to an Executives Requires B.A. Implements programs and policies Designs and Plan Relies on experience and judgment to accomplish goals Salary + Bonus	0-3 years experience Works under supervision May require B.A. Has knowledge of commonly used concepts. Relies on instructions and pre-established guidelines Commission only or salary + comm. For headhunters salary is usually a percentage of placed clients salary.	3-5 years Reports to Executive Requires B.A. Previous management or sales rep experience Relies on sales ability Salary + comm

11% of permanent positions are obtained through staffing and temporary agencies. While that seems like a low number, that is actually great considering the purpose for which they exist. They exist to help you with a temporary solution for a temporary timeframe, with an average assignment lasting 2-4 weeks. For some the purpose of both the Recruiter and the Staffing agency is to provide the best talent, to the best company for the best price.

As you progress in your career, be careful of agencies that request you to revise your qualifications for a position as opposed to finding a position that suites your current qualifications. This is not the best source for job seekers. The likelihood of this agency being able to place you is slim which is why they are asking you to delete or add experience.

In order for them to place you and pay you a decent rate, they have to downgrade or upgrade your skill set. Choose an agency that will represent you well and allow you to put your best foot forward. When staffing agencies ask you to revise or downgrade your resume "for a position" - ask why.

Do not confuse the above statement with an agency offering constructive criticism designed to assist you with improving your résumé. I am speaking specifically of agencies that may request you to add skills you don't have to be placed or take off skills you do have so that you can be placed. Yes, this happens. While doing market research I had a staffing agency to request I delete six (6) years of experience so that I would not "look" over qualified for a position they would like to submit me for. Taking off six (6) years would have made me appear to be a five-year generalist instead of the 11-year human resource professional that I was at the time of the incident.

This was obviously not a career fit for me as I had more experience than the company would need and probably would have been unhappy, unchallenged and unfulfilled. An additional six years of experience can be the difference between a Supervisor or Jr. Executive and an Executive or Sr. Executive depending on the structure of the organization. Be careful, remember the job search is about you, your accomplishments, your story, and revolves around your success. Your goal is to take steps forward...not go backwards.

It is important for job seekers to understand the differences so they can make the best choices when needed to rely on others to present employment opportunities. It is essential for the job seeker to know the purpose of the source to which they leave their credentials.

While all three are viable sources for the job seeker, they each have their own purpose. As a job seeker, you have to utilize the source that best fits your career goal. As a job seeker, you have an advantage with the HR Manager, Recruiter and staffing agencies. You can accept or reject any offer extended - based on the tasks, criteria, locations and pay.

The information provided is not to stray a job seeker from using staffing agencies, recruiters or headhunters, but to educate job seekers on the processes by which they choose the best resource for their career plan. There is a difference between being efficient (doing things right) and being effective (doing the right thing). Regardless to the source, all job seekers want to be placed in a position where they are promotable.

Why Should I Hire You?

Section 19
I am promotable

PROMOTABLE - the ability to move forward and advance in stations, rank or honor.

Approximately 10 years ago, I completed a course on "Becoming a Promotable Woman". This course was given by the National Businesswomen's Leadership Association. Even though some of the topics covered were geared specifically towards women, the lessons learned were invaluable for anyone who wants to be promoted.

The introduction of the course described the profile of the a promotable woman as:

THE PROFILE OF PROMOTABILITY

1. An achieving person (ambitious - aggressive).

Be productive - do 10% more than others and at a higher quality, learn to brag about it to let others know.

2. A High level of motivation

Motivate yourself - watch people who are succeeding and mirror what they do.

3. Identification

Have your own style and make sure that people see you and what you do.

4. High degree of individuality.

Be yourself like yourself and magnetize others

5. Strong sense of self-esteem

Know who you are and don't budge.

These areas of promotablity are important in order to build lateral relationships and gain support from people who are not your supervisors. In a study conducted by the Center of Creative Leadership research shows men are promoted on potential (vested interest) and women are promoted on performance (proven ability).

This study further showed there are essentially three levels of promotablity. Take a moment to examine each and discover where you are in your career.

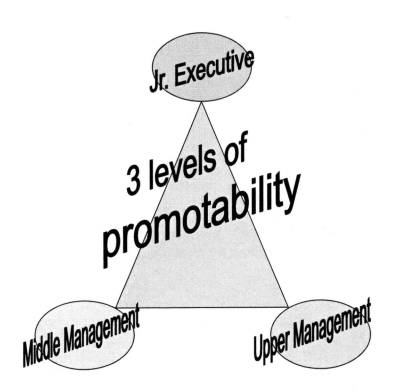

Jr. Executive (5-7 years)

Acquire skills and expertise, experiments learn the political ropes, rapid promotions or lateral promotion.

Middle Management (7-10 years)

Implementing and sharpening management skills. Where area of expertise is expanded and fine-tuned. Expand and fine tone leadership through communication and people skills.

Upper Management (10 years plus)

Breaking into the boardroom - utilizes executive mastery of all levels of business and the ability to make effective strategic decisions about an organization's future.

In upper management you are the leader or visionary, no longer managing people, but inspiring others to do their best pulling everything together for cohesiveness. There is more to consider that just the monetary aspect of your new "position". You know have the lives of other people in your hands. Be sure that you consider everything that comes with your territory, now other's are depend on you.

Leader
A person who has commanding authority or influence.

Visionary
Having or marked by foresight and imagination.

There is a difference between being a leader and a visionary. To state it simply, anyone can see how it can be done (or offer an opinion about it). But not everyone can accomplish the tasks to get it done.

We have all known someone who stayed in the EXACT same position, for many years without promotion or an opportunity for promotion. Even though they were probably a very good workers, great communicators, loyal employees, etc, - the reason they lack promotion is the ability to possess leadership skills or the ability to be a visionary.

A good leader must possess vision. To have vision, you must be able to lead. The reality is this, it is your vision and no one else can see your vision so you must possess the ability to lead them to it. When an employer is looking for a leader there are 8 general areas to be considered. Making the transition between the two is often a mindset. Here is a list to help you discover and tap into your inner strength. Focus on developing these during the Jr. Executive stage.

VISION
TRUST (confidence)
INSPIRATION (motivation)
COMPASSION
INFORMATION
EMPOWERMENT
INTEGRITY (character)
RECOGNITION

Source: The Conference on Leadership Development & Team Building

When an employer can clearly see that you have both leadership and visionary abilities, they are less inclined to go outside of the organization to find the missing piece in the puzzle.

Why Should I Hire You?

Section 20

I Am The Missing Piece To The Puzzle

Puzzle - to attempt a solution by guesswork or experiment.

Have you ever put together a jigsaw puzzle? There are many pieces to choose from but only one will be a perfect fit. Even when there is an attempt to force the pieces together, at times the pieces look like a perfect fit, until they are placed in position. This same is true for job seekers.

This segment is a bonus for those of you who may not be seeking a new employer, but rather seeking to be promoted within a company. Time to tap into your career strategies. The career search does not end when you are offered a position with a company, in fact, it's only the beginning. The ability to be promotable within any organization begins with how the job seeker unites with his or her employer on day one.

It's up to you (job seeker) to show the employer who is hiring for an administrative assistant that you can manage the office. It's up to you Jr. Executive to convince the employer that you are management material, you just need a little mentoring.

Let's explore a few career derailments:

- **Failure to utilize networking opportunities -**

Networking within an organization is the best strategy for a promotion. Have you ever worked with someone who appeared to always know what was going on and offers reliable information? It is possible because they have built relationships with people outside of their departments. People in other departments come to know them as a resource and are willing to give and receive information from them.

Networking is a powerful tool. There's no mystery to it, you just have to build relationships wit people can help you reach your goals. Make sure that in return, you have something to offer.

- **Failure to do more than their job description -**

There is always one. If my written job description has four items on it, they say "I'm doing those four things and no more". With an attitude of such, it's a set up for failure. If you will not do more than what is required in your current position, you will not be considered for positions requiring more responsibility and accountability.

Employers want to see you master the small areas before they entrust you with a larger area. You can do it, but you have to have a willing spirit (and others must see it) so that they will want to include you in projects.

- **Failure to toot their own horn –**

If you believe you can do the job - say it and then prove it. Speak up and ask for the additional responsibility (be prepared to do the work without complaining or asking for a raise until your review) Time out for being looked up as a kisser-upper or brown nose. Who cares? While you are being promoted, they will still be in the same position, complaining.

Confidence in your ability is key. If you never ask for the job, you may never be considered. This is not permission to brag or boast on your skill or ability, but an opportunity to share wit others - more of the fabric you are made of.

- **Failure to be seen with the "right" crowd -**

It is common to walk into an organization and see "those who look alike" with each other. It is okay to want to have lunch and work with people whom you are most comfortable with. But can you adjust when you are the minority? Don't get caught up thinking you have to hang with a certain group, department or shift. The last thing you want to do is hang with the person who the company President doesn't care for. When a car is repossessed - you don't get to pick out your personal belongings, the car and everything associated with it, is at a loss. The company president is the repo-man, and you are the possession in the car. Take a look around the parking lot and see what car you are driving. Examine your workplace relationships. Are you seen with people who have promotion or potential inside of them?

Whether you are seeking an internal promotion or a promotion by way of a new employer, remember the ten creeds of promotability. The ability to be promotable speaks in volume for your accomplishments.

131

10 Creeds of Promotability

1. **KNOW THYSELF -**
   Understand your strengths and weaknesses and assess yourself.

2. **BE ABLE -**
   Have technical ability, people skills and Good Health.
   The future you go up the more energy it takes.

3. **BE VISIBLE -**
   Be Visible and seen as able (advertise your achievements) on print and in person. Send thank you notes

4. **RELY ON OTHERS -**
   Network

5. **PREPARE TO RECEIVE -**
   Others will contact you.

6. **TAKE CONTROL OF YOUR CAREER -**
   Ask for what you want and need

7. **LEARN THE POLITICAL ROPES -**
   Know who has the real power in the organization

8. **NEVER STOP NETWORKING -**
   Internally and Externally and Volunteer

9. **KNOW WHAT YOU WANT -**
   Know when your goals change and when to prioritize.

10. **GO FOR THE BOTTOM LINE -**
    The company bottom line is to make a profit (make it yours also)

Part 6
Paid What I'm Worth

Why Should I Hire You?

Section 21
My accomplishments speak volume

Accomplish - something completed or attained successfully

This statement allows the job seeker to "toot their own horn". Making such a statement requires that you have something to back up what you say. If you are just beginning your career, START COLLECTING ALL YOU CAN. Build a portfolio to ensure it speaks to your accomplishments.

What should go in your portfolio?

Everything that backs up what you say (résumé, letters of reference, newspaper clippings, awards, transcripts, special recognition, certifications and training certificates). Anything career related that would show tenacity, determination and knowledge at a particular subject. Why? It stands on its own merit.

It is not necessarily an accomplishment to "just" belong to a civic organization. Many people pay for the membership and never utilize the benefits or get involved in the cause. Many pay for the membership without an understanding of the features and benefits. To fact that you belong to social and professional organizations look great on your credentials if you are not active, it can come back to haunt you. Unless you have made a significant contribution to an organization, do not list it in your credentials as an accomplishment. As a job seeker, unless you are active in the organization or making significant contributions, it may be better to make it known you are not active. You don't want to sit on the other side of the desk of someone who called you in for an interview because you are a part of the same organization - only to find out she is the membership chair and can't find your name on the roll.

Let's take a moment to examine the two words closely.

Goal - a purpose or objective.

Accomplishment - Something successfully achieved.

A goal is only an objective of something you are setting out to do, while your accomplishment is something you have successfully achieved.   Your goal in only an objective something you are setting out to do, while your accomplishment is "successfully" achieved.

Knowing the difference between the two can save you a lot of embarrassment.   With so many wonderful, yet different industries to explore - accomplishments, which stand out, make the difference in how a company values your employment.

For example, if I were attempting to be an Employment Services Professional for a local college, it would benefit the company for me to belong to an association, which other employment or college professionals are also members. Belonging to a sorority or fraternity in this instance, would not be as beneficial.

Here are a few examples of how job seekers list goals as opposed to accomplishments.

GOALS	ACCOMPLISHMENTS
Joined a civic organization	Served as Board Member for a civic organization
Graduated from college	Graduate Cum Laude
Hired as Store Manager	Only woman manager in division
Completed filing assignments weekly	Created Intranet to house all corporate forms
Wrote a book of poetry	Published #1 selling book of poetry
Volunteered for catering event	Organized catering event for 500 people
Worked for a Fortune 500 Company	Promoted within company twice in 1 year

There are many benefits to becoming a part of professional and social organizations.

Here are a few that I enjoy as a member of the National Résumé Writers Association:

- Access to pertinent industry specific information through newsletters, publications, conferences and workshops.

- Mentoring programs that will help to match with seasoned professionals.

- Expert's Corner providing support groups where members are willing to share their expertise with other who need advice of specific topics.

- Monthly online chats that offer feature speakers and a variety of topics with time for Q&A.

- Annual conventions, monthly workshops, conferences, and meeting with opportunities to meet colleagues both locally and nationally.

- National PR and exposure than many generate exposure and leads.

- Membership discounts that vary by organization.

- Opportunities to volunteer and get involved and a sure way to get connected.

Section 22
I am Connected

**Connected - having social, professional or
commercial relationships.**

As you can see, there are many features and benefits to
holding memberships when you are active and accountable.
In the appendix of this book, I have listed several business and
trade organizations that help members with employment
assistance.   Providing just one more reason to make an
investment in your career.   The bottom line is PEOPLE HIRE
PEOPLE!

As I was establishing my agency, one of the first things I looked
for were people to help me reach my goals. I selected my
Board Members based on the goals in my business plan. For
each segment of my business plan, I found someone in that
industry that was "connected".   I am connected to them and
they are connected to their industry, which makes me
connected as well. When the time comes for you to utilize your
connections, people have to know whom you are to speak on

your behalf.   I also want to point out there is a difference between being "connected" and getting the "hook-up".

When you are connected, you work to meet your goals with the assistance of your connections as alliances. When you look for a hook-up, you are asking people to do something for you - for nothing. One of the areas that perplexed me when I began my agency was people who thought I was enough of the "expert" to seek my services, but thought I should give them away free.   After all "I am the President, I can make that decision"...is what they said.   Giving away free services defeats the purpose of being in business.   I would politely ask "how can I grow my business if you won't support it?"

Here's another reality: many job seekers get lax when a friend or family member has an inside connection to a job offer. For some reason, they feel they don't need to do as much to obtain the position.   That is 100% incorrect.   If for no other reason that to show appreciation for the person who informs you about the connection, your should go the extra mile, to not only make yourself look good, but them as well.

I would like to pause here and share an encouraging story about the benefits of being connected. Several years ago, I completed a 6-month women's economic development course. During the graduation ceremony a speaker shared an invaluable lesson with the graduates. Long before she opened a business, while she was still working on a job she did not enjoy, she began attending functions in the industry to which to she aspired to be a part of. She set aside a certain amount of her paycheck to pay the entrance fee to the various functions sponsored by the industry (she was not a member of any of the organizations).   Through her persistence and determination, doors began to open for her several years before her "planned Grand Opening".

Positioning herself to became a regular attendee at industry events, people began to inquire "who she was". She kept herself in front of the right people and made connections. The day of her Grand Opening, she was fully supported by the decision makers in her "new" industry.   People she had developed a relationship with while building her business. This made here eligible to ask for letters of support that enabled her to gain funding, access to contracts, and other things she needed to be successful in this "new industry"

View the following as suggestions to make a place to become a job seeker who is connected:

Volunteer

This shows that you have passion for what you do. Surely, if you will task for free, you will enjoy it more for pay.

Join Organizations

Many people turn to organizations to inquire "do you know anyone who...?

Research

Find out what is coming down the pike and avail yourself.

Talk to people

Meet people outside of your circle, social comforts and department.

Attend gatherings

Do not leave until you get what you came for - connections.

After the event, make a point to stay in contact with the people you have connected with. It would be a shame to do all that work and never use it to your advantage. When you begin to talk, people listen. Make sure the buzz surrounding you is positive. There are many ways to place your credentials in from of potential employers by utilizing others. When you have more than one source to choose from, you give yourself options.

Section 23
Weight the Options

Options: the power or right of choosing.

To invest or not to invest, that is the question? Your right to choose has a huge impact on your career search. Uncle Sam wants you to work. You are worth more to him when you are employed. The good thing is some of what you invest in tax deductible.

During the last leg of this book, an everyday conversation sparked this section. In this conversation a job seeker was inquiring as to how much pampering she would receive at a local spa for $100. (I told her right then, I am going to write about you in my book!). The reason this is of significance in this same person has contact me a few prior for career planning and development price points. We set up a consultation and discussed her career aspirations, how I could help and the cost that she would incur. Immediately, her focus became cost. She was in agreement that she needed the services and that it would help her to advance in her career, but she was not willing to invest the money into her career.

She was currently employed and the best time for her to invest would have been while she was gainfully employed. What would it have cost her? Taking a bag lunch for a few weeks, saying no to a new pair of shoes, or possibly her $100 day of pampering at the spa.

Approximately one year after initially talking with this individual, her résumé surfaced in my inbox - same resume, same employer, still job seeking. Why? She did not fully weigh her options, prepare or make the investment. Yes, she had her day at the spa - which did absolutely nothing for her career.

I believe there was a lesson to be learned in sharing that story.

- Job seekers do have resources for the investments they choose to make.

- Job seekers are in control of their career search. Having the right to choose which investment to make is critical - but only effective when the right choice is made.

- The next lesson learned is the perfect time to look for another position is while you have one.

It may not be the position you desire, but it certainly provides you with the means to make an investment in your career. Purchasing this book (thanks!) and reading the contents will do you no earthly good id you do not apply the principles and lessons within the book.

There is a difference between making a living and living your life. What are the differences, I'm glad you asked. INVESTMENT AND PREPARATION! The first step of preparation is to make an investment in what is important and will produce a return.

Finding the resources (cash) required to invest in your career must be a priority for anyone seeking a career as opposed to a job. The investment now works for you in the long run. How? Many investments are tax deductible - even when you are technically unemployed, self-employed or doing side jobs to make ends-meet.

If you are looking for a career in your current profession, you can itemize some of your deductions. Employment agency fees, resume preparation, printing, phone calls, miles driving to and from the interviews, and mailing expenses are examples of deductible items. The expenses for an out-of-town interview are deductible items when you have to pay for them.

Is there anything else tax deductible?

According to Jackson-Hewitt there are many overlooked or forgotten employment expenses that would otherwise tax liabilities.

- Use of car for business travel on business

- Entertainment of business expenses

- Career related educational expenses

- Seeking a new position in your field

- Moved expenses incurred sue to a new position

- Working from home

- Purchases for your businesses

For a full list view www.jacksonhewitt.com

How to itemize and apply this to your search?

- Dance instructor - deductions include records and tapes used for classes.

- Psychotherapist - deductions include cost of personal-growth seminars in order to evaluate their suitability for your client is deductible. Yes, facial tissues that your clients use as well.

- Sales - deductions can include meetings in your home, the coffee you serve and paper cups are write offs, if you hold meeting in your home.

- Wardrobe consultant - deductions include cost of mirrors in the office.

- Journalist - deductions include daily newspapers.

- Swimming teacher - deductions include swimming lesions given from home.

- Professional speaker - deductions include audio and video equipment.

Other employment/business expenses can include:

Bank service charges
Books and periodicals - related to your industry
Business conventions - even those on cruise ships
Career counseling
Electronic mail services
Office supplies
Operating loss from the previous year (new business)
Passport fees for business trips
Professional and trade associations (network to your next position)
Postage and shipping
Printing and duplication
Check with your local CPA or Financial Accountant to see which items are tax deductible for your individual situation.

Unfortunately, recent graduates are out of luck for deductions. The cost you incur getting your "first job" are not tax deductible. There is a difference between a job and career. Never stop learning - just remind yourself that career continuation is a lifestyle for a lifetime.

Section 24
Career Continuation

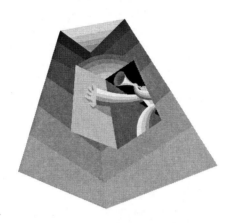

Continuation - something that continues, increases or adds.

Believe it or not, job seeking is a full time job. A serious job seeker will commit to a minimum of 25 hours per week for active job seeking. It takes that much effort of more to achieve your desired results. Just as you are tracking your tax-deductible expenses, a job seeker should also log the time spent seeking. Several things can come out of tracking what you do.

- You will see methods, which are responsive, and those that are not.

- You keep yourself busy and motivated.

- You maintain focus on what needs to be done.

- You keep accurate dates of progress.

- You will avoid the tendency to become lazy.

How you organize your job search is critical to ensuring that you see immediate results. Your career-planning specialist can assist you with the best plan, but in the meantime, use this as a guide:

7:00am	Eat breakfast, Shower and get dressed for an interview. This way if an opportunity arises, you will be able to go immediately.
8:00am	Gather necessary tools for your job search • Telephone • Copy of résumé • Target computer sites • Paper and pencils • Newspapers • Yellow pages • Connection contacts (business cards) • Thank you notes and stamps
9:00am	Begin calls to connection contacts who are expecting your call/ follow up with old leads.
10:00am	Contact new prospects (this gives an employer time to arrive and handle office business before the phones start ringing)
11:15am	Take a break
11:30am	Get out of the house, drop of résumés in your area.
1:00pm	Contact leads form newspapers, organizations, job boards, placement offices, etc.
1:30pm	Take a lunch
2:00pm	Surf the internet to gather leads for tomorrow's search
4:00pm	Track your progress.

What to do while making phone calls:

- Email and fax copies of your résumé to potential employers and indicate that you will be calling this afternoon. Give a specific time.

- Look for industry specific sites to submit résumé.

- Post your résumé online (this can take 30 minutes per site).

- Prepare thank you notes for people you have interviewed with or made positive contacts with.

- Make copies of your résumé.

- Search the Internet for companies in your industry and prepare driving directions.

Why Should I Hire You?

Section 25

Unproductive Cycles

Unproductive - opposite of yielding results, benefits or profits.

Cycle - an interval of time during which a sequence of a recurring succession of events or phenomena is completed.

While preparing the book, I spend many hours researching and compiling market research. To ensure the goal of the book (educating job seekers) is carried out, it is equally important to share all of the information founded - both positive and negative.

For job seekers to be fully educated in the employment process, it is necessary to share things in the employment process which man not be fruitful for everyone's career path. Of course, I am not trying to make anyone look bad, but I am bringing to light some challenges that may exist for job seekers.

Every agency or organization will not fit into your career plan. They simply will not be beneficial to the job search process. It is important for job seekers to understand both sides to determine and apply the best strategy for their individual career goals.

- **Head hunters**

Headhunters are an excellent source for providing leads. The draw back with using a headhunter is that you rarely have the opportunity to develop a relationship with them. They are submitting your résumé and 20 other applicants' for the same position. The object is the get the best employee in front of the employer. Usually an employer is bombarded with many résumés and eventually choose one they want to interview. The more résumés the headhunter can place before the employer, the better the chances are for an employer to choose one of their candidates.

This not always going to be the best career option for everyone. Especially a job seeker who needs to find employment today.

- **Staffing/ Temporary Agencies**

Some state agencies provide a "one-stop" approach intended to beneficial for active job seekers. It's an excellent source for those who need access to computers, job leads, workshops, résumé reviews, etc. Here are some challenges I found in my research.

- o <u>Computers</u> - time limits that prevent you from fully taking advantage of the job search online. If you are posting your résumé on computer sites, one entry can take up to 30 minutes. It would require you to be at the state office 3 times in one week if you wanted to post to 3 separate sights.
- o <u>Workshops</u> - limited resources. I asked for a copy of the booklet presented to a job seeker in a career workshop and was surprised that the facilitator asked, "why did I want the book?" I told him I was unable to attend the workshop but wanted to preview the materials. He gave me the book, yet never inquired if I could attend the next session beginning in 20 minutes. I asked him how long had he worked for this state agency and what was his background in the career services field. He told me that he had graduated from college and majored in computer science, however, he had a desire to be a

public speaker so he asked to start doing career workshops.

- o Job Leads - My research showed that most job leads were old, outdated and already filled. The process of selecting 3 jobs and submitting your résumé and waiting for a state agency employee to get back to you to decide if you had the experience and skill level BEFORE allowing you to apply for the position took several days. I also found that many of the requests I made, I received emails indicating that I lacked experience in specific areas. Which was strange considering, I put together mock résumés that included the requirements. I found myself emailing several times (the same résumé) before it was accepted. This process was also limited to only being able to select 3 jobs leads per week.

- o Job leads via the Internet - a 3-to-4 day turn around to receive contact information (after I already emailed for several days). By the time you are able to obtain the information on the position, it could take over 2 weeks. The position is now old.

- o Résumé Reviews (this was my FAVORITE!). Indeed it was a success story (ha!). I had contact an agency to see if someone could give me pointers on my résumé. Since I am a professional résumé writer, I had taken in one of my original formats - which I had intentionally made grammatical errors to. The person who reviewed my résumé was so taken by my résumé layout that she did not notice all the mistakes. I asked her how she had received her job. She told me she was "welfare to work" success story. This was the first job she had ever had, she had been in her position for 6 months and only had to take a 4-hour class on résumé writing. Again, I was floored.

- **Copy centers**

The individual hired to create résumés is a graphic artist and not a human resource professional or even a person trained to read a résumé. It can be detrimental to your career to have a great "looking" résumé that says nothing.

I strongly encourage job seekers to have a professionally written résumé. It is an investment that can change your career and your life. I also caution job seekers to ask questions about the credential of those writing résumés.

I was invited to present for a national résumé association and was surprised at how many résumé writers had NEVER worked in an environment allowing them to gain the perspective of a human resource professional. Many were prior housewives, social workers and people who just heard it was good money.

Granted, I thought it was a great accomplishment to see so many résumé writers attend a conference where they would be educated on "what human resource professionals want to see". I believe that anyone who spends a considerable amount of time in a position should garner experience from it; you would be surprised at how many résumé writers on the internet offer "guarantee's" that they can not back up. Remember the purpose of the résumé is to get you an interview, not a job. Stay away from résumé writers who promise you a job if they write your résumé.

It's worth every penny to pay for the expertise of someone recognized in their field as an expert. Some career planning services can become expensive, but remember, you are not always paying for the "service", but rather the "expertise" gained by utilizing the service. This can be the difference between your job (odd or occasion piece of work) and your career (continued progression in any career).

If you found this book to be informational, give us a call. Of course we provide the career services you are seeking. Our passion is to educate job seekers and the last 16 years have been spent being educated in this field.

Before sending out another résumé consider the following:

- Does your résumé say anything significant?

- Does your résumé stand out in the stack?

- Does your résumé list great words, but lack power?

The question WHY SHOULD I HIRE YOU? is not merely a simple question. It is quite complex. It is a power packed question that should summarize, your ability, your success, your desires and ultimately tell your story.

Part 7

Features and Benefits

Section 26
Features and Benefits

Why Should I Hire You?

Product/Service	Feature	Benefits
Youth Workshops	Workshops designed for youth outlining economics, leadership and self-esteem.	Prepares youth for "real world" issues relating to career readiness and life enhancement skills.
Career Workshops	2-hour workshops designed for job seekers that cover: Understanding the Recruiting Process, Power In Presence, and Getting Paid What You're Worth.	Prepares job seekers with hiring techniques from the perspective of human resource professionals and what they are trained to look for when seeking potential hires.
Resu-Cards ™	Pertinent information from resume on a business card.	Highlights a job seekers skill level and fits into the 20-second resume review rule. Provides job seeker with a networking strategy.
Customized Resumes	Customized to Profile the candidate	Prepared by Human Resource Professionals Differentiates from other candidates List Duties and Accomplishments Qualifies Candidate Opens the door to new opportunities Shows the employer a level of professionalism
Custom Cover Letters	Customized to profile the candidate. Can provide salary information	Prepared by Human Resource Professionals. Differentiates from other candidates. List Duties and Accomplishments Qualifies Candidate Opens the door to new opportunities Shows the employer a level of professionalism
Salary Analysis	Shows the client their value and worth Points out total compensation package as viewed by the employer.	Helps the client understand the employer view. Shows the client their market value. Enables the client to successfully negotiate a salary
Salary Report	Provides market compensation data specific to industry, geographic region and company size.	Market Data: benchmark job, base pay, total compensation. Company Data: how to set pay, raises and promotions. Personal Outlook: personal variables Worksheets: Preparing for a raise, new job or promotion, negotiation pointers.
Internet Posting	P.H.D. Staffing does the research. Places client resume on the Internet	Stays online for 1 year. Puts clients in front of prospective employers works for you while you work for others
Jobs by Fax	Client resume faxed to 15-50 employers	Resume is faxed to companies who have current openings

Part 8
Appendix

Section 27
Associations online

Section 28
End Notes

Section 29
About the Company

Section 30
About Author

Section 31
Upcoming Projects

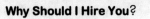

Why Should I Hire You?

Why Should I Hire You?

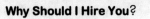

Why Should I Hire You?

162

APPENDIX

Professional and Trade Associations to consider. Most offer career assistance for members. Non-members can also pay an entry fee for networking events.

Industry	Website	National Number
Accountants	www.smallbizaccountant.com	201.573.9000
Administrative Professionals	www.naessa.com	703.237.8616
Advertising	www.atlantaadclub.com	800.999.2231
Auditors and Accountants	www.theiia.org	407.830.7600
Benefits Professionals	www.webenefits.org	414.821.9080
Black Accountants	www.nabaatl.org	301.474.6222
Black Data Processors	www.bpda.org	301.429.2702
Black MBA Association	www.bmba.org	312.236.2622
Building Owners and Managers	www.boma.org	202.408.2662
Business Economics	www.nabe.com	202.463.6223
Business Marketing	www.marketing.org	800.664.4262
Clergy Executives & Administrative Assistants	www.aceaa.org	770.761.0592
Commercial Real Estate (women)	www.crewnetwork.org	404.471.1110
Contract Management	www,ncmahq.org	800.344.8096
CPA's and non CPA's	www.aicpa.org	212.569.6299
Creative Club	www.creativeclub.org	404.874.0908
Customer Service	www.icsa.com	800.360.4272
Employee Benefits	www.ifebp.rg	414.786.6710
Financial Executives	www.fei.org	201.898.4600
Financial Services (women)	www.fwi.org	703.807.2007
Fundraising	www.portal.afpnet.org	800.666.FUND
Graphic Artist	www.aiga.org	212.807.1990
Health Nurses	www.aahon.org	770.455.7757
Heating, Refrigeration, Air conditioning	www.ashrae.com	404.636.8400
Human Resources (African Americans)	www.naaahr-atlanta.org	404.755.5846
Human Resources Planning	www.hrps.org	404.836.2200
Information Technology	ww.itaa.org	703.522.5055
Lawyers (women)	www.lar.emory.edu/gawl	404.656.2382
Legal Secretaries	www.nals.org	918.493.3540
Logistics Engineers	www.sole.org	800.695.7653
Marketing Professionals	www.smps.org	703.549.6117
Marketing Related	www.ama.org	800.262.1150
Mechanical Engineers	www.asme.org	800.843.2763
Meeting Planners	www.mpi.web.org	972.702.3000
Non-profit	www.nonprofitgeorgia.org	404.688.4845
Performance Improvement	www.ispi.org	202.408.7969
Planning	www.planning.org	312.431.9100
Production and Inventory Control	www.apics.com	800.444.2742
Project Management	www.pmi.org	610.356.4600
Public Administration	www.aspanet.org	202.393.7878
Public Relations	www.iabcatlanta.com	800.776.4222

Public Relations	www.prsa.org	212.995.2230
Quality Administrators	www. asqc.org	800.242.1946
Real Estate	www.corenetglobal.org	800.726.8111
Records Managers and Administration	www.arma.org/hq	800.422.2762
Retired Officers	www.troa.org	703.549.2311
Safety Engineers	www.asse.org	847.699.2929
Sales and Marketing	www.SME-Atlanta.org	678.432.0803
Society for Human Resource Management	www.shrm.org	703.548.3440
Strategic Leadership Forum	www.strategicleadershipforum.com	800.873.5995
Supply Management	www.napmga.org	602.752.6276
Technical Communication	www.stc.org	703.522.4114
Training and Development	www.astd.com	800.626.2783
Women Accountants	www.awwa.org	800.326.2163
Women in Communications	www.womcom.org	800.974.1979
Women In Construction	www.nawic.org	800.552.3506

For a full listing of local chapters, meeting times and benefits offered, view the websites or call the national headquarters and speak with membership services. For state and federal agencies, contact your local phone book.

End Notes

In order of appearance

<u>Harold J. Bell</u>
Page IX - Career Continuation is a lifestyle for lifetime™

<u>Merriam Webster's Collegiate Dictionary tenth edition, 1993,
Merriam-Webster, Incorporated</u>

All Chapter Definitions

<u>Human Resource Management Eighth Edition - John M.
Icavcevich, 2001, McGraw-Hill Irwin</u>
Page 10 - What is Human Resource Management?
Page 10 - What is the function of Human Resource
Management?
Page 10 - How is Human Resource Management Measured?
(emphasis added)
Page 13 - Domestic Model for Human Resource Management
Page 14 - Job Analysis
Page 14 - Steps in the Job Analysis process

<u>The Work Book - Getting the Job You Want, J.Michael Farr,
Richard Gaither, R. Michael Pickrell, Fourth Edition, Glencoe,
Macmillian/McGraw-Hill 1987</u>
Page 22 - Here a few tips to remember: (emphasis added)

40% of job seekers remain unemployed because of poor
appearance. The way you look, the way you behave, the way
you write, the way you speak (emphasis added)

<u>Drake Beam Morin</u>
Page 28 - 6% of management positions are obtained through
any Internet site as opposed to 61% obtained through
networking.

Spherion Pacific Enterprises LLC , 2003
Page 28 -_7% of positions were obtained through any Internet board
Page 43 - A study by Spherion Pacific Enterprises, showed 12% of people
Page 90 - Job referral sources
Page 110 - Best times to reach candidates
Page 111 - Here are the top five reasons - Disqualifying categories

Eliston Word Processing Plus
Page 30 - How to write an effective email (emphasis added)

TypeFocus, Inc.
Page 42 - According to test administered by TypeFocus®

Personal Best, Inc. - research by Founder and President, Peggy Newfield
Page 49 - 62% body language, 28% tone of voice, 10% words

Psychology of Color by David Johnson
Page 54 - Psychologically speaking, let's take a look at what your colors may be saying (emphasis added)

Becoming a promotable Woman, Sally Briggs Jenkins, 1990
Page 58 - Other levels of competencies (emphasis added)
Page 121 - The Profile of Promotability (emphasis added)
Page 122 - Three levels of promotability (emphasis added)
Page 127 - 10 creeds of promotability chart (emphasis added)

Development Dimensions International
Page 59 - Targeted Interviewing Techniques (emphasis added)

www.salary.com
Page 67 - Position description and salary info for Paralegal

Iceberg analogy by Dick Berry
Page 90 - What is the iceberg anology?

What's in a C-A-R-E-E-R? by Stephanie C. Harper - published by
The Challenger Newspaper
Page 96 - What's in a C-A-R-E-E-R? (emphasis added)

Black Enterprise, Annual Careers and Opportunities Issue,
February 2004, Research by DevahPager, Northwest University
Page 104 - Workplace Discrimination

Occupational Information Network
Page 113 - Human Resources
Page 114 - Recruiters
Page 114 - Staffers

Source Unknown at time of print
Page 117 - 11% of positions are obtained through staffing and
temporary agencies.

The Conference on Leadership Development and Training, Skill
Path Seminars.
Page 123 - Here is a list to help discover and tap into your inner
strengths

Jackson-Hewitt - employment expenses
Page 141 - According to Jackson-Hewitt, here are a few
overlooked or forgotten employment expenses.

P.H.D. Career Strategies - Company Business Plan
Page 152 - Features and Benefits

Internet Public Library
Page 155 - List of Online Associations by Society of Association
Executives
(emphasis added)

National Résumé Writers' Association
Page 132 - Summary of Benefits (emphasis added)

All information herein is believed to be accurate and reliable.
However, neither the author nor P.H.D. Career Strategies
assumes any responsibility thereof. Correction requests should
be mailed to P.H.D. Career Strategies, Book Corrections, P.O.
Box 54166, Atlanta, GA 30308.

About The Company

P.H.D. Career Strategies is an agency specializing in preparing job seekers.   We offer an array of career services including: workshops, résumé- writing, success coaching, human resource consulting and training for those who want to transition from Expert (in their field) to Entrepreneur.

In our offices:

- We were created with the job seeker in mind.

- We are certified human resource professionals.

- We don't practice preparing job seekers, we specialize in it.

When it comes to career strategies

We conceive them

We cultivate them

We support them

We make them work.

For your career needs, give us a call, we would love to be your career planning and development specialists.

The office of Stephanie C. Harper, PHR, CCP, CHRM
P.O. Box 54166, Atlanta, GA 30308
404.299.8757 / info@StephanieHarper.com
www.stephanieharper.com

Board Members

Harold J. Bell
Director
Career Planning and Development
Spelman College

Chiquita Board
Extension Educational Agent
University of Georgia - Cooperative Extension Agent

Marcellus Jackson, JD
Director
Economic Development Center
Clark Atlanta University

Mildred Mason
Director
Abundant Joy

Vivianne Hardy Townes
Business Strategist
VHT Business Strategies

Leutrell M. Osborne
Exective Director
Community Development Director

Rev. Josephine Williams
Board of Directors
First Ladies Incorporated

(past members - yet still advising)

Velma W. Larkins

Administrator (retired)

About the Author

A California native, Stephanie has over 16 years experience in Administration and Human Resource Management. A recognized career expert and invaluable resources to the career services field, she is much sought after for her expertise. The Association of Clergy Executives and Administrative Assistants, Association of Job Search Trainers, Atlanta Business Chronicle, Department of Labor, Federal Aviation Administration, National Resume' Writers Association and the University of Georgia are just a partial list of organization which have sought her services.

Stephanie is the founder of a career planning and development agency located in Atlanta, Georgia. The agency is uniquely designed to educate, empower and employ job seekers and assist organizations with process to best align organizational goals with human assets.

Stephanie has carved out an indelible mark in the career services field and is a regular contributor to radio shows, national publications, career conferences, business groups and worship centers. She also has a nationally syndicated career minute with broadcasts to more than 2.5 million listeners on a weekly basis.

A graduate of both MTI Western Business College and Columbia Southern University, she has furthered her education to include the following certifications: Professional in Human Resources (PHR), Certified Compensation Professional (CCP), and Certified Human Resource Manager (CHRM).

A woman with a servant's heart she volunteers with many community and faith-based organizations. Stephanie also teaches dance and sign language to youth ages 2-15.

Other Projects by Stephanie C. Harper include

EXPESSIONS

Other Projects by Stephanie C. Harper includes:

Expressions

A Book of Poetry by

Stephanie C. Harper

Stephanie C. Harper is an author, career expert and speaker. Author of WHY SHOULD I HIRE YOU? and A KINGDM BUILT CAREER, she is a published author who contributes regulary to radio shows, national publications, career conferences, business groups and worship centers.

www.stephanieharper.com
www.whyshouldihireyou.com

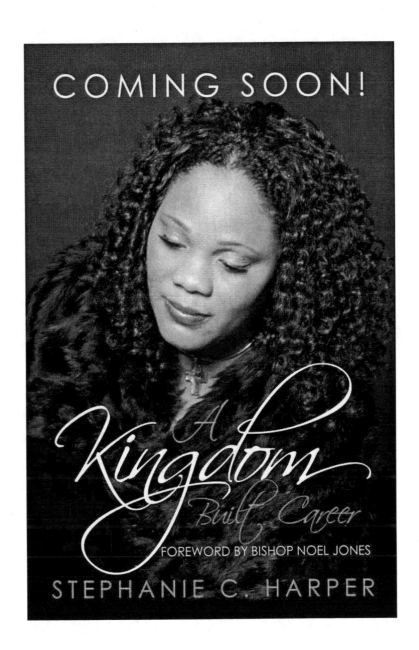

COMING SOON!

A Kingdom Built Career

FOREWORD BY BISHOP NOEL JONES

STEPHANIE C. HARPER

(Expected Release Summer 2005)

Preface

Have you spent 40,000 hours with God? Each year we spend over 2000 hours in the work place allowing people, economics, attitudes, perceptions, and images to determine our destiny. Let's assume the average person has a 20-year work life span. That is more than 40,000 hours spent putting together the pieces of the work place puzzle - the thing we trust to shape our lives. Your career is by extension, your life. Your career is often associated with identity, satisfaction, and at times a sense of mourning, but rarely associated with Christ.

Perhaps we should spend less time planning, preparing, and educating ourselves on how to have a successful career and more time planning, preparing and educating ourselves on finding our purpose. What is purpose you ask? Purpose is not what you do, but what you are willing to die for. Can you honestly say that you have spent equal time becoming a success as perceived by the world as you have dying to self to become who God called you to be?

Are we are so busy building our ideal career that when God needs to speak to us; we are preoccupied? The priority becomes meeting deadlines, preparing the big presentation, making the sale, securing the elite client, and becoming the consummate professional, that we forget kingdom principles established in the Word designed to teach us and give us a promise we can hold on to.

Could it be the will of God to use the layoff to show Himself as the provider? Would God use interview after interview to challenge us to confess our strengths and weaknesses? Are we positioned to counsel workplace conflict to be a beacon of light? Is the difficult boss a test of our ability to submit to authority? Surely, these could not be the steps required by God for success.

How does one measure success? Success is not measured by prestige, position, pay, popularity, promotion or people. Here comes the shocker. God did not call us to be successful. God called us to be obedient. Through our obedience God will bring opportunity to talent. Success is living and walking in the will of God, positioning is a result of His will for us. The time to seek God for direction is not at the hurdle in our career, but daily so He can bless our career with His provision. Having a kingdom built career first requires being who God called us to be. That is success defined and a career that gives God glory.

Thank you for your time, support and interest.

Let us know if the information provided
has been useful to your job seeking strategies.

We would love to hear from you.
Please print out the attached form or send
your comments, questions or observations to:

P.H.D. Staffing Strategies
P.O. Box 54166
Atlanta, GA 30308

For more information on Career Strategies,
please visit us on the web at
www.phdstaff.com
or
whyshouldIhireyou.com

Resources

The "P.H.D. Perspective™"
(Original career articles by Stephanie C. Harper)
2002 © 2003 ©
Published by GreaterDiversity.com

Merriam Webster's Collegiate Dictionary - Tenth Edition
Merriam -Webster Incorporated - 1993 ©
Thomas E. Stanley, Publisher

Human Resource Management - Eight Edition
John M. Ivancevich - 2001 © McGraw-Hill/Irwin

The Promotable Woman - Leadership Series
Sally Briggs Jenkins - 1990 ©
National Press Publication

Business Grammer and Usage for Professionals
Communication Series
Kathy Bote - 1992 ©
National Press Publication

The Workbook - Getting the Job You Want
J, Michael Farr, Richard Gaither, R. Michael Pickrell
Glencoe Publishing Company 1997 ©

Working from Home
Paul and Sarah Edwards
G.P. Putnam's Sons

Job -vs- Career

Webster defines the two as such

Job
to do odd or occasional
pieces of work

Career
A field for or pursuit of consecutive
"progressive" achievement.

Successful Career Management is more than just
following a cookbook list of sequential behaviors.
Career Management is about changing behaviors for
improved results. Career Management ensures that
you have exposure to leadership development,
performance, productivity, training and career
development.

Ask yourself, what's in a C-A-R-E-E-R?

C   Choices
A   Assessment
R   Research
E   Explore
E   Execution
R   Responsibility